Making Love for Her:

A Companion Book to Making Love for Him

Intended to Instruct and Remind Women

About the Important Roles They Play

In the Lives of the Men

Who Love Them

By

Mary L. Seager, MS, LPC

Dedication

I dedicate this book to each woman who may read and attempt to follow the instructions contained herein. Striving to be the best she can be, to make of her dreams a reality, and to meet the needs of others around her is a great and noble calling and a quest from which she must not shrink. Hers is the backbone of society, and strengthening herself cannot but aid the cause of all who look for her to show the way.

—Mary Seager

Contents

Foreword

Making Love for Her is a companion book to *Making Love for Him* and is intended to instruct and remind women about the important roles they play in the lives of the men who love them. Women are the mothers, the sisters, the daughters, and wives, whose tender and compassionate influence carries their male counterparts onto greatness within their own specific realms. Each man and woman is a special being who can touch the hearts of many and bring about much good. It is the good that a woman can do in the life of a man, especially as his life's partner, that is the focus of the work that follows. As she learns to serve him, she serves her own better interests by shaping his finer qualities, endearing him to her unendingly, and teaching him to assist in promoting her own wellbeing and that of her children. *Making Love for Her* is meant to strengthen *her* position in *his* life, thus, strengthening her overall and endowing her with the ability to win a great victory in their relationship, that of being complete with his love to sustain her and enduring their mutual trek across time.

In her quest to attain and protect the love and adoration of her chosen life's partner, a woman must learn to embrace and exemplify the finer qualities of womanhood, with which she has naturally been endowed. She must also fashion and uphold a lifestyle that will draw to her those with whom she can comfortably relate, including the man of her dreams. In addition, she must know of the place which *she* holds in *his* life and of the many roles she performs therein. It is by being the best she can be that she engenders within him a desire to do likewise. Also, it is by creating a life of her own that she creates a life she can share with others. Additionally, it is by accepting the role of womanhood that womanhood becomes all it was meant to be, a place most supreme in the lives of those who look for her to show the way, to meet their needs, and to provide a haven wherein they may safely dwell, protected from all life's storms.

Chapter One

"Who Can Find a Virtuous Woman?"

Who can find a virtuous woman? for her price *is* far above rubies. The heart of her husband doth safely trust in her, so that he shall have no need of spoil. She will do him good and not evil all the days of her life. She seeketh wool, and flax, and worketh willingly with her hands. She is like the merchants' ships; she bringeth her food from afar. She riseth also while it is yet night, and giveth meat to her household, and a portion to her maidens. She considereth a field, and buyeth it: with the fruit of her hands she planteth a vineyard. She girdeth her loins with strength, and strengtheneth her arms. She perceiveth that her merchandise *is* good: her candle goeth not out by night. She layeth her hands to the spindle, and her hands hold the distaff. She stretcheth out her hand to the poor; yea, she reacheth forth her hands to the needy. She is not afraid of the snow for her household: for all her household *are* clothed with scarlet. She maketh herself coverings of tapestry; her clothing *is* silk and purple. Her husband is known in the gates, when he sitteth among the elders of the land. She maketh fine linen, and selleth *it;* and delivereth girdles unto the merchant. Strength and honor *are* her clothing; and she shall rejoice in time to come. She openeth her mouth with wisdom; and in her tongue *is* the law of kindness. She looketh well to the ways of her household, and eateth not the bread of idleness. Her children arise up, and call her blessed; her husband *also,* and he praiseth her. Many daughters have done virtuously, but thou excellest them all. Favour *is* deceitful, and beauty *is* vain: *but* a woman *that* feareth the LORD, she shall be praised. Give her of the fruit of her hands; and let her own works praise her in the gates (Proverbs 31:10-31).[1]

Webster[2] describes *virtue* as an "inherent power to produce effects; potency." Outlined within the above passage of scripture are means by which a woman can wield great power and influence in the life of a man. He considers the example she sets in determining his own courses of action. He also looks to her as the principal source through which many of his needs are met. In addition, he knows she will strengthen and uphold him in facing all life's challenges placed before him.

What is a woman unto a man? She is his mother, his sister, his daughter, his wife. She nurtures him, befriends him, looks to him as a primary means through which her needs are met, and loves him. Without a woman, a man's life is a mere shadow of what it could be. She is the warmth, the color, the flavor, and sweet aroma of his existence. Her laughter fills his heart. She is his joy in times of gladness, his solace in despair.

---

[1] Corporation of the President of the Church of Jesus Christ of Latter-Day Saints. (1979). *The Holy Bible.* Salt Lake City, UT: The Church of Jesus Christ of Latter-Day Saints.

[2] Kellerman, D. F. (1975). *New Webster's Dictionary of the English Language* (College Ed.). New York, NY: Delair Publishing Company, Inc. The reader is referred to this citation for all subsequent mention of Webster.

She will never leave him, *or should not*, saving for the greatest of offense. His heart can "safely trust in her" as the firm foundation upon which he continues to build his own character as a man, adds to and strengthens the bulwark of their union, and affords others the blessing of their companionship as, together, they establish and maintain friendships and other family ties.

His Heart "Doth Safely Trust in Her."

What does it mean for a man to trust in a woman? Webster defines *trust* as a "reliance on the integrity or justice of a person or confidence in some quality, feature, or attribute of a thing; confident expectation or hope." He also indicates that *to trust* is "to have faith or confidence in something or someone; to hope," "to have trust or confidence in; to rely on; to believe; to allow to be somewhere or do something without fear of consequences," and "to expect confidently or to hope." Therefore, for a man to trust a woman means that he is confident in the uprightness of her conduct both when they are together and when they are apart, that he does not doubt the steadfastness of her loyalty and devotion as his partner over time, and that, despite challenging circumstances, he knows she will be a constant source of love and support for him.

Why is trust such an important element in a relationship, especially that between a man and a woman? I believe it is because most of us have had our hopes dashed at some point in one relationship or another and that the positive expectations we may have possessed at the outset of our lives must then be renewed through fresh and uplifting experiences. That is where the woman of each man's dreams plays a most important role. He knows his heart can safely trust in her, and she must never disappoint him. He has been hurt before. Now is the time of his solace and rejoicing. By way of example, my husband and I, both having been wounded in relationships from the past, embarked upon our union with a fair amount of trepidation. Therefore, it was most important for us to be constant in our mutual love and devotion. Otherwise, one of us or the other may have been immeasurably and indefinitely harmed by coming to see relationships as being even more dangerous than we had known them to be before.

The Book of Ruth well describes the attitude a woman must possess in regard to abiding with the man who holds her dear. She could well say unto him, as Ruth said unto her mother-in-law, Naomi,

> Intreat me not to leave thee, *or* to return from following after thee: for whither thou goest, I will go; and where thou lodgest, I will lodge: thy people *shall be* my people, and thy God my God: Where thou diest, will I die, and there will I be buried: the LORD do so to me, and more also, *if ought* but death part thee and me (Ruth 1:16-17).[3]

The words of Boaz unto Ruth are also a fitting summation of how a woman must treat the man who loves her:

> Hearest thou not, my daughter? Go not to glean in another field, neither go from hence, but abide here fast by my maidens: *Let* thine eyes *be* on the field

---

[3] *The Holy Bible.*

that they do reap, and go thou after them: have I not charged the young men that they shall not touch thee? and when thou art athirst, go unto the vessels, and drink of *that* which the young men have drawn (Ruth 2:8-9).[4]

Naomi's words unto Ruth further confirm that truth. She said, "*It is* good, my daughter, that thou go out with his maidens, that they meet thee not in any other field" (Ruth 2:22).[5]

At Naomi's instruction, Ruth lay at the feet of Boaz and said unto him, "I *am* Ruth thine handmaid: spread therefore thy skirt over thine handmaid; for thou *art* a near kinsman" (Ruth 3:9).[6] Boaz' answer unto Ruth proved the wisdom of Naomi's counsel. He replied,

Blessed *be* thou of the LORD, my daughter: *for* thou hast shewed more kindness in the latter end than at the beginning, inasmuch as thou followedst not young men, whether poor or rich. And now, my daughter, fear not; I will do to thee all that thou requirest: for all the city of my people doth know that thou *art* a virtuous woman (Ruth 3:10-11).[7]

Ruth remained constant to those things which she knew to be true. The steadfastness of her behavior, in addition to her expressed desire that Boaz take her as his wife, endowed him with the confidence necessary to honor her in marriage, to care everlastingly for her

---

[4] *The Holy Bible.*
[5] *The Holy Bible.*
[6] *The Holy Bible.*
[7] *The Holy Bible.*

needs and those of her mother-in-law, Naomi, and to give them a son, one whose posterity would reign over all Israel. Who can question the merits of developing trust as a virtue among women?

Truths that can be gleaned from reading the account of Ruth and her courtship with Boaz revolve around characteristics of devotion and honor, both of which played important roles in the formation of a union that history would later revere. Made of similar substance was my maternal grandparents' relationship with one another. As a young dating couple, their courtship was put to the test and proven to be true when, on one occasion, Grandma was approached by some acquaintances and asked to accompany them on an outing which was to include both male and female parties. Grandma declined the invitation, and Grandpa, upon hearing of her refusal, perceived her devotion towards him and honored her with a further level of commitment in their own union.

How might a couple today emulate characteristics from the past that have bred for positive relations between men and women throughout history? Observation and consideration are fundamental to understanding and developing those traits which we hope to incorporate into our own lives. Below is an exercise intended to assist in that regard and to instill within a process to be followed again and again as one makes the journey toward self-improvement and the betterment of one's circumstances.

In considering some of your own observations and life experiences, what examples of trust in women's relationships with men come to mind? Those may include, but are not limited to, interactions between parents, grandparents, aunts and uncles, neighbors, and friends.

_____

_____

_____

_____

_____

_____

_____

_____

_____

How do you, as a woman, develop trust in your life and in your interactions with the men you know?

_____

_____

_____

_____

_____

_____

_____

_____

_____

In what ways do you perceive you might improve?

_____

_____

_____

_____

_____

_____

_____

_____

_____

How might those improvements enhance your life and your relationships?

_____

_____

_____

_____

_____

_____

_____

_____

_____

Verily I say, [wo]men should be anxiously engaged in a good cause, and do many things of their own free will, and bring to pass much righteousness; For the power is in them, wherein they are agents unto themselves. And inasmuch as [wo]men do good they shall in nowise lose their reward (D&C 58:27-28).[8]

According to the definition in Proverbs, a virtuous woman is anxiously engaged in doing many good things and in strengthening herself physically and in every other way through her continual endeavors. A woman of Biblical times of necessity gathered in the materials needful to make yarn and fabric and honed the essential skills to clothe herself and her kin. A woman adept at working with textiles produced beyond the needs of her own family and bartered with the excess in procuring other goods requisite to maintaining her household. Those may have included foods that could not be obtained elsewhere. Her loved ones did not suffer from cold or hunger for meat. She gleaned produce from her own field, planted with her own hands. Her arms and body were strengthened through her diligent efforts.

Modern-day women are not so different from ancestral females. We, too, must work for a living, and, while many of our day-to-day activities take us from our realm of home and family, home and family still

---

[8] Corporation of the President of the Church of Jesus Christ of Latter-Day Saints. (1981). *The Doctrine and Covenants of the Church of Jesus Christ of Latter-Day Saints.* Salt Lake City, UT: The Church of Jesus Christ of Latter-Day Saints.

reign supreme among the callings of importance in our lives. We, too, must see to the basic needs of our loved ones as we gather our "food from afar" in providing sustenance for them, as we clothe them with the finest apparel our incomes can afford, and as we strengthen our minds and our bodies to enhance longevity and quality of life. It is our intention to live long and well with those who depend so heavily upon us and to create an existence that will bring us everlasting joy. Not unlike women of olden times, a woman in today's society who looks well to meeting the needs of her household will be well loved by her children and her husband alike. They will rise up "and call her blessed," and "her own works [shall] praise her in the gates."

Of all the blessed women I have known, whose works may "praise [them] in the gates," my maternal grandmother stands forth as being a most shining example of womanhood. I remember the care she offered her family in preparing for them meals and other delicacies they would remember throughout their lifetimes. My mother spoke of the homemade cakes Grandma used to make for her and her older brother when giving them tea parties as small children. My oldest brother simply would not give up on finding her recipe for chicken soup after her passing. That was always a family favorite. I remember the beef roast and brown gravy and boiled potatoes and carrots from the garden she had awaiting me following the birth of my daughter and upon our arrival home from the hospital. I can't recall tasting anything quite as flavorful as Grandma's cooking. Everyone loved her dill pickles, mustard pickles, and chili sauce. Strawberry, raspberry, and blackcurrant jams, carrot pudding with lemon sauce, fruit cakes, and honey cookies enlivened our hearts throughout the holidays and long winter months. Nothing from Grandma's garden went to waste as long as there were jars in which to preserve the fruits and vegetables that grew so plentifully therein.

Cooking was a most important virtue in my grandmother's household, as my grandfather had suffered from digestive-tract problems throughout his life and needed the utmost care in maintaining the health and strength required to run a family business and to provide the necessary means to support his loved ones in comfort and with a certain amount of flair. Grandpa contributed to the bounty of their table as well by raising cows for milk and beef and chickens for meat and eggs and by tending to his garden, the showplace of the neighborhood, as his most beloved pastime. He loved and appreciated my grandmother for the love and care she tirelessly offered him, their children, and grandchildren. They were a great pair in working side by side to accomplish their most meaningful tasks in life, caring for one another and all whom they cherished.

One point of interest is that the plot of land where my grandparents raised their chickens was purchased by my grandmother with some money her mother had given her when she was newly married. The Book of Proverbs speaks of how a virtuous woman "considereth a field, and buyeth it." My grandmother could obviously hold her own with women of old on that account. The many grapevines Grandma had growing in her yard could also constitute a vineyard, planted "with the fruit of her hands."

In regard to textiles, my grandmother always had an eye for fashion, though she had to work very hard in her youth to earn the money necessary to purchase the clothing and accessories she desired. In her married years, her hands were endlessly working to crochet doilies for the adornment of her home, to embroider pillow cases, which would later be passed on to posterity, and to sew aprons, which no well-bred housewife would be seen without in her day. Clothing construction and repair were among her highly valued talents in ensuring her family members were presentably dressed to meet the public and to engage in their various walks of life and the social functions of their day. My grandfather could not have helped but be "known in the gates, when he [sat] among the elders of the land," or the local businessmen of the area. Furthermore, my mother and her older brother were not unlike the lord and lady of a fine manor in their well-attended state of dress and grooming. My grandmother was the heart of her home and the love of her family's lives for the love and care she offered through her many endeavors.

As pertaining to strengthening her mind and her body, my grandmother's active lifestyle and focus on nutrition allowed her to live to the ripe old age of 98 years. Though her abilities to care for the temporal needs of her family diminished over time, she remained a constant source of love, support, and encouragement through her abiding presence in our lives to the very day she passed from among us. The example she set is one we can all follow in lengthening our days and enlivening our minds.

Developing balance in life is an important concept when it comes to being anxiously engaged, or living life to its fullest. Caring for one's health, or physical wellbeing, through proper rest, exercise, nutrition, and sometimes medical management is an aspect that cannot be denied our utmost attention. In addition, one's mental, emotional, and spiritual needs are of great importance and similarly deserving of our focused concentration. While not each of those life areas is a topic that will be addressed in the work at hand, each is, nonetheless, worthy of the reader's consideration and may be thought of as a focal point for being anxiously engaged in her own life and in the lives of others.

In considering some of your own observations and life experiences, what examples come to mind of women who are anxiously engaged in doing much good in their lives and in their relationships with the men they know? Those may include, but are not limited to, interactions between parents, grandparents, aunts and uncles, neighbors, and friends.

_____

_____

_____

_____

_____

_____

_____

_____

_____

How are you, as a woman, anxiously engaged in doing much good in your life and in your interactions with the men you know?

_____

_____

_____

_____

_____

_____

_____

_____

_____

In what ways do you perceive you might improve?

_____

_____

_____

_____

_____

_____

_____

_____

_____

How might those improvements enhance your life and your relationships?

_____

_____

_____

_____

_____

_____

_____

_____

_____

"Her Candle Goeth Not Out By Night."

Another virtue of womanhood is *her* ability to engender within *him* a sense of security and belonging through the physical love she offers. It has been said that a man feels love through the physical union he shares with his partner.[9] That is one means by which a woman can love a man, *one that is most important to him.* What may be forbidden in certain realms outside of marriage is wholly sanctioned within. I have known of women who struggle to grasp that concept. A young married woman had confided in me that she, having come from a highly religious background and having been raised by a father who was a leader in his church,

---

[9] Gray, J. (1995). *Mars and Venus in the Bedroom.* New York, NY: HarperCollins Publishers, Inc.

15

had been taught to shun physical intimacy before marriage and continued to do so afterwards.

Remaining in a state of celibacy certainly has its merits for one who is unwed, especially in today's society. Avoiding sexually transmitted diseases and unwanted pregnancies, in addition to retaining a sense of self-worth and self-respect at having adhered to one's own value system, are immeasurable rewards for maintaining one's chastity and purity. However, after a woman has knelt at the altar and given herself to her husband, as he has given himself to her, another set of priorities takes shape. He and she are now to be as one in their physical union as well as in all other aspects of their conjoint lives. A sexual relationship, in addition to being a vehicle for enhancing the pleasure a man and a woman can enjoy together, is a means of procreation and of bonding between husband and wife. It is a symbol of their love and a frequent and necessary reminder of the vows they spoke at marriage. They are for one another and for none else. That is in token of their promise to abide with one another faithfully to the end.

The Apostle Paul counseled, "*Depart* ye not one *from* the other, except *it be* with consent for a time, that ye may give yourselves to fasting and prayer; and come together again, that Satan tempt you not for your incontinency" (1 Corinthians 7:5).[10] Paul was fully aware of the unrestrained passions and sexual appetites to which we, as human beings, are held subject. In God's wisdom, one sex is drawn to the other in His great plan of procreation, and marriage is a fitting place

---

[10] *The Holy Bible.* – Joseph Smith Translation added

wherein physical intimacy may be expressed and experienced completely. That which at first seems to be a weakness of the flesh becomes strength when a man and a woman are united in God's plan.

At the outset of their relationships, many couples may be relatively inexperienced in engaging in physical intimacy, and, while some may naturally or readily adapt to including sexuality in their marriage unions, others may struggle with self-concept or degree of comfort in becoming sexually active with their partners. In such cases, it may be wise for husbands and wives to discuss their concerns with one another or to seek advise through either religious or secular leaders in the field of counseling or through family members or friends who have been proven to be good listeners or to offer wise counsel. Many books have also been written on the subject of developing mutually satisfying sexual relationships, and the prior citation by John Gray may be considered one of the best among them. Being open with one another about their concerns and searching out the opinions of experts or the advisement of loved ones cannot but aid a couple in pursuing their quest for sexual happiness.

One or two exceptions may exist to making oneself fully available in meeting the sexual needs of one's companion. Those would simply be a lack of physical or emotional health and wellbeing for one partner or the other. Some women may experience frequent infections or other physical-health problems that may prohibit them from engaging in intercourse or other sexual activities until such maladies may be remedied through proper medical interventions. Advanced stages of pregnancy may also interfere. Other women may suffer emotional trauma related to sexual activity and stemming from a history of abuse. The emotional needs of those women may take precedence over the sexual needs of their partnerships, and resolution of those difficulties may have to be achieved through counseling or other means before a satisfying sexual relationship can be attained. In addition, sexual dysfunction for both women *and men* may stem from a combination of physical and emotional problems. In cases where physical or emotional concerns may prevent a couple from experiencing full sexual satisfaction through intercourse, other means may be employed to meet the needs of one's partner. For example, partner-assisted masturbation is an acceptable method of enhancing the pleasure inherent in a marriage union and may be considered an alterative to intercourse under certain conditions and at specified times.

In considering some of your own observations and life experiences, what examples come to mind wherein strong physical bonds have enhanced relationships between men and women? Those may include, but are not limited to, interactions between parents, grandparents, aunts and uncles, neighbors, and friends.

_____

_____

_____

_____

_____

_____

_____

_____

_____

How do you, as a woman, if in a committed relationship with a man, apply a strong physical bond in your life and in your interactions with him?

_____

_____

_____

_____

_____

_____

_____

_____

In what ways do you perceive you might improve?

_____

_____

_____

_____

_____

_____

_____

_____

_____

How might those improvements enhance your life and your relationship?

_____

_____

_____

_____

_____

_____

_____

_____

_____

"She Reacheth Forth Her Hands."

A woman who is mindful of the needs of others around her is a choice gift in the life of her husband. Not only is she attentive to his wants and those of her children, but she is sensitive to all who come within the realm of her helping influence. There are many who lack so much in this life, those without mother or father, sister or brother, son or daughter, husband or wife. A gentle touch in the life of one who stands in need does not go unseen by the watchful eye of one who intends to "plant his affections"[11] in noble ground. Embedded in the book of Ruth is a beautiful illustration of that point. Ruth, in response to Boaz' kindness to her, knelt before him and asked, "Why have I found grace in thine eyes, that thou shouldest take knowledge of me, seeing I *am* a stranger" (Ruth 2:10)?[12]

> And Boaz answered and said unto her, It hath fully been shewed me, all that thou hast done unto thy mother in law since the death of thine husband: and *how* thou hast left thy father and thy mother, and the land of thy nativity, and art come unto a people which thou knewest not heretofore. The LORD recompense thy work, and a full reward be given thee of the LORD God of Israel, under whose wings thou art come to trust (Ruth 2:11-12).[13]

Where in history have more handsome words been spoken than those of Boaz in showing forth his appreciation unto Ruth for the care she offered a near kinswoman unto him? What greater reward could he bestow than giving unto Ruth a lifetime of continual companionship and constant care? Her kindness unto her mother-in-law did not go unnoticed or unrecompensed.

My own mother, who passed away recently, is also a noble example of one who has shown forth love unto others through her constant care. She has stretched out

---

[11] Doran, L. (Producer), & Lee, A. (Director). (1995). *Sense and Sensibility* [Motion Picture]. United Kingdom: Columbia Pictures.

[12] *The Holy Bible.*

[13] *The Holy Bible.*

her hands in meeting the needs of many, including those who were strangers to her. I remember a story she told me about responding to a knock on her door and finding on her doorstep a man who expressed a desperate need. "Please help me. I'm starving," were his pitiful words. Her response to him was to offer in abundance the bounty of her kitchen. She prepared for him a meal that would sustain him until his needs could be met more fully and lastingly elsewhere. Though he knew nothing more about my mother than her first name and perhaps did not even know how to find his way back to her home, he later discovered a means by which he could express his appreciation. One day, as my mother was looking through the local paper, her eyes fell upon a personal ad that read, "Thank you, Lorraine. You saved my life." Could that expression of gratitude have come from any other source than the man who came knocking at my mother's door? Perhaps it could have, but the likelihood is that my mother did save his life or at least enhanced it measurably. How could we, as her family, allow to be unnoticed the kindness and the giving nature that were so profoundly hers? Such characteristics certainly merit the reward of our everlasting love and devotion both in mortality and beyond the grave.

Looking beyond one's own needs in meeting the needs of others is a point so beautifully illustrated in the Book of Ruth as well as in the life of my mother. It is also a characteristic worthy of emulation and for which many a man might be seeking as he pursues his quest for companionship in this life. In developing the qualities necessary to be of assistance to others, it is essential that one be watchful in gaining an awareness of others' wants and responsive in taking the necessary actions to meet their needs. As was the case with my mother and the man she found awaiting her on the doorstep, opportunities may come to us without our striving to find them, and simply being open and willing to assist are the attributes necessary to bestow acts of kindness. However, as in the case of Ruth and her mother-in-law, Naomi, not all who stand in need are quite so willing to ask for our help. For those who are relatively unacquainted with that story, it should be pointed out that Naomi tried to discourage Ruth from following after her into the land of Judah after both their husbands had died. While being careful not to offer offense, at times, like Ruth, we must be diligent in pursuing after others that we might overtake them in their plight and bestow our benevolent will. Again, being watchful and responsive, open and willing, and diligent in our pursuit are often necessary that we might be the "saviors of men" (D&C 101:39-40;[14] 103:9-10)[15] in our sojourn on earth.

In considering some of your own observations and life experiences, what examples come to mind in which women have cared for the needs of others, including those of the men they knew? Those may include, but are not limited to, interactions between parents, grandparents, aunts and uncles, neighbors, and friends.

_____

_____

_____

---

[14] *The Doctrine and Covenants of the Church of Jesus Christ of Latter-Day Saints.*
[15] *The Doctrine and Covenants of the Church of Jesus Christ of Latter-Day Saints.*

_____

_____

_____

_____

_____

_____

How do you, as a woman, care for the needs of others in your life and in your interactions with the men you know?

_____

_____

_____

_____

_____

_____

_____

_____

_____

In what ways do you perceive you might improve?

_____

_____

_____

_____

_____

_____

_____

_____

_____

How might those improvements enhance your life and your relationships?

_____

_____

_____

_____

_____

_____

_____

_____

"In Her Tongue is the Law of Kindness."

The Book of Proverbs suggests that a virtuous woman exercises both wisdom and kindness in choosing the words she speaks. Webster indicates that *to be wise* is to have "the power of discerning and judging correctly," to be "possessed of discernment, judgment, and discretion," to be "prudent; sensible;

judicious; sage," to have "extensive knowledge," to be "learned; shrewd." *Wisdom* is defined as "the quality of being wise; the faculty to discern right and truth and to judge or act accordingly; sound judgment; sagacity; discretion; common sense; extensive knowledge." *To be kind* is to be "of a good or benevolent nature or disposition," "proceeding from a good-natured readiness to benefit or please others," "beneficent, helpful, friendly, or cordial," "pleasant, agreeable, or favorable." *Kindness* is defined as "the state or quality of being kind; benevolence; a kind act; an act of good will."

The Bible, though primarily a patriarchal account, contains numerous depictions of women whose wisdom and kindness, both in word and in deed, have made them heroines for all time. Their noble examples have altered the course of history and greatly impacted the lives of the men who were fortunate enough to know them and to love them. For instance, King David would have made a fatal error in destroying the household of Nabal, a man who "*was* churlish and evil in his doings," had it not been for the intercession of Nabal's wife, Abigail, who "*was* a woman of good understanding, and of a beautiful countenance" (1 Samuel 25:3).[16] Nabal had foolishly withheld his bounty from David in refusing to feed him and his men after they had offered protection to his shepherds. It was, therefore, David's intention to destroy Nabal and all that pertained unto him. Fortunately, one of Nabal's young men, knowing the wisdom and the kindness of Abigail, informed her of the matter and entreated her to mediate in behalf of her household. She, therefore, sent

---

[16] *The Holy Bible.*

provender to David and his men and met them in the way.

Abigail, knowing David to be a man of greatness, lighted off the donkey she rode upon and knelt before him. She expressed grief that Nabal had treated David and his men so disparagingly and took blame upon herself and her ignorance of their needs that food had not been sent more readily. She asked David to disregard the unkindness of her husband and declared her knowledge that David was favored of the Lord and that one day he would rule over all Israel. She petitioned him to forgive her trespass and to remember her in the day he would be king. David gave thanks unto the Lord for preventing him from destroying Abigail's household and unto her as well for offering her timely advice. He accepted the gift of food she bestowed upon him and his men, and later, after Nabal had died, he again thanked the Lord and sent word to Abigail to take her unto him as his wife.

Abigail's wisdom and kindness saved herself and her household from utter destruction and won her a place of honor in the Kingdom of David, but she was not alone in standing bravely for the things she believed in and knew to be true. Esther is, yet, another example of a woman whose virtue shone brightly through the wisdom and the kindness of the words she spoke (The Book of Esther).[17] Her beauty and other virtues had found favor with Ahasuerus, the king of Persia and Media, so that he made her his queen. She was of Jewish heritage, of those who had been taken captive and carried away from Jerusalem by Nebuchadnezzar,

---

[17] *The Holy Bible.*

King of Babylon, and was the adopted daughter of her cousin, Mordecai. Yet, the king knew nothing of her lineage or family ties until one day, at the prompting of Mordecai, she risked her life in approaching the king with her petition that he save her people from their planned destruction by Haman, a prince most highly favored in the kingdom of Ahasuerus. Her request met with the king's approval, and his anger was kindled against Haman. He granted her people the opportunity to defend themselves against their enemies, and thousands of his subjects met their deaths as they attempted to stand against Mordecai and others of Jewish descent.

Both Abigail and Esther showed forth wisdom and kindness in bringing providence into the lives of their households and their people through the words they spoke and the influence they had on the great and powerful men in their lives. Among the virtues of womanhood, wisdom and kindness, both in word and in deed, are certainly not the least. A woman may need to stop and think, or offer sound consideration, before she speaks or takes action. She must employ the time necessary to weigh the relative impact of what she is about to say or what she intends to do prior to following through on her impulses. In that way, she may very well be taking an important step in developing the wisdom and the kindness she seeks as she moves forward in her numerous interactions with others in the world around her.

In considering some of your own observations and life experiences, what examples come to mind in which women have exercised wisdom and kindness, both in word and in deed, in their lives and in their relationships with the men they knew? Those may include, but are not limited to, interactions between parents, grandparents, aunts and uncles, neighbors, and friends.

_____

_____

_____

_____

_____

_____

_____

_____

_____

How do you, as a woman, exercise wisdom and kindness, both in word and in deed, in your life and in your interactions with the men you know?

_____

_____

_____

_____

_____

_____

_____

_____

_____

In what ways do you perceive you might improve?

_____

_____

_____

_____

_____

_____

_____

_____

_____

How might those improvements enhance your life and your relationships?

_____

_____

_____

_____

_____

_____

_____

"She riseth . . . while it is yet night" "and eateth not the bread of idleness."

Through the scriptures, we are counseled,

Cease to be idle; cease to be unclean; cease to find fault one with another; cease to sleep longer than is needful; retire to thy bed early, that ye may not be weary; arise early, that your bodies and your minds may be invigorated (D&C 88:124).[18]

According to Proverbs, a virtuous woman "riseth . . . while it is yet night" "and eateth not the bread of idleness." If she is to accomplish the many tasks of womanhood and make something meaningful of her life, it is imperative that she utilize her time and her energies most wisely. After all, both time and energy are limited resources.

Though I may grumble about getting out of bed more mornings than not, my current work outside the home requires that I arise before dawn and invest considerable amounts of physical and mental energy in fulfilling the duties of my job. It is only in the mid-afternoon, after my workday is done, that I can return home to tasks, both physical and mental, that are awaiting me there. Dirty dishes and laundry seem never ending. Clutter and dust won't often give me a

---

[18] *The Doctrine and Covenants of the Church of Jesus Christ of Latter-Day Saints.*

break. Shopping and meal preparation are also on my daily agenda. Thank goodness for my husband, who willingly lends a hand with those! Though my daughter is grown, she lives only a short distance away with two little ones of her own and another one shortly forthcoming. While her husband has been a great support to her, she is also in need of my help and that of my husband. Speaking of my husband, he, too, expects a little attention every once in awhile, and who can blame him for that? With so much to do on a daily basis and so many needs to fulfill, I have a difficult time imagining how I might while away the hours or get overly much sleep. It's how to go about getting enough rest that's a more constant worry on my mind, but, as busy as I may be, I love what I do and know the pleasure and satisfaction of a job well done.

As a single woman living alone with my daughter some years ago, I found that making the best use of my time and energies was of the utmost importance in accomplishing a most meaningful task. I had a deadline to meet in completing a master's thesis. Such an undertaking required a great amount of self-direction and discipline, and engaging in casual pursuits and lounging in bed simply were not "in the cards"[19] for me at that time in my life. The scriptures teach us "that by small and simple things are great things brought to pass; and small means in many instances doth confound the wise" (Alma 37:6).[20] It was through "small and simple" means that I developed the necessary

---

[19] origin and meaning cited on www.phrases.org.uk/meanings
[20] Corporation of the President of the Church of Jesus Christ of Latter-Day Saints. (1981). *The Book of Mormon: Another Testament of Jesus Christ.* Salt Lake City, UT: The Church of Jesus Christ of Latter-Day Saints.

perspective to treat my thesis project as though it were a fulltime job. That motivating factor allowed me to arise early each morning, drop my daughter off at school, work a full day at the computer lab at my university prior to retrieving my daughter and returning home to face the responsibilities awaiting me there, and then do the necessary reading and writing to prepare for my next productive workday at the computer lab. Following are some "small and simple" words that came to mind in the form of a poem I would repeat over and over again as I found it necessary to rekindle the flame of desire to progress from day to day with my work at hand.

SLUGABED

Slugabed, get out of bed.
Don't be such a sleepyhead.
You can't go on counting sheep
If you want to earn your keep.

Slugabed, don't rest your head.
If you want your family feed,
You'll just have to mend your ways,
Make good use of longer days.

As inane as it may seem, that *Mary Goose Nursery Rhyme* saw me through a year of dedicated endeavor in completing my thesis and my degree and in moving me closer to gainful employment that would open doors of opportunity in other realms of my life as well. By simple means were "great things brought to pass."

My favorite story about the merits of arising early to make good use of time and energies was told to me

33

by my maternal grandmother. It was about my maternal grandfather and took place just prior to his meeting and falling in love with Grandma. Grandpa had left his boyhood home and family of origin in the country to find work in the city where Grandma lived. A friend had accompanied him on his journey and in his quest for employment. Grandma loved to tell of how Grandpa arose early and found a job and about how his friend slept in late and failed to procure one. That's a simple illustration of how "the early bird catches the worm."[21] However, it meant far more than that to my grandparents. It was through my grandfather's employment in that city that he was able to meet and marry my grandmother and through his characteristic approach to life, arising early and "putting his best foot forward,"[22] that he remained a constant provider years after others of his generation had sought retirement. What worked for my grandfather in his relationship with my grandmother also worked for me in getting to know my husband, as I will recount in an upcoming chapter.

What are some motivating factors that may prompt a person to arise at dawn and "put his or her best foot forward" in pursuit of his or her life's goals? The poem I used to illustrate my own source of motivation in completing my master's thesis falls in line with certain cognitive principles, or the notion that our thoughts influence our actions and our feelings. Aaron Beck is often credited as being the father of that particular mode of therapy, though others, including Albert Ellis, may have preceded him in developing

---

[21] origin and meaning cited on www.phrases.org.uk/meanings
[22] origin and meaning cited on www.phrases.org.uk/meanings

those theories. Even the writer of Proverbs attested, "For as [a man] thinketh in his heart, so *is* he" (Proverbs 23:7).[23] Also, it was David Burns, a student of Aaron Beck, who brought cognitive therapy into public view with his popular writings.[24]

Other strategies used to spur one to take action may fall in line with more purely behavioral principles. One may merely perceive the long-term reward inherent in taking certain actions. For example, if I do my homework, I "make the grade."[25] Therefore, I do my homework. However, there does seem to be an undeniably cognitive undertone even to the purest of behavioral strategies. Furthermore, one may develop a token-reward system to keep oneself motivated while pursuing a long-range goal. For instance, I may give myself a smiley-face sticker for every 10 pages of reading that I do for my American-history class. For every 10 stickers, I get a Snickers bar. Therefore, I work my hardest to get those smiley faces *and those Snickers bars*. Hopefully, by so doing, I will also gain the ultimate reward of doing well in my American-history class.

The same principles can be applied as we pursue our goals in life, those which carry us beyond an academic or similarly contrived setting. My poem would be just as beneficial, apart from my scholastic endeavors, in inspiring me to make the best use of my time and energies in fulfilling work commitments or household chores. I can see the benefit of working hard

---

[23] *The Holy Bible.*
[24] Burns, D. D. (1980). *Feeling Good: The New Mood Therapy.* New York, NY: Signet.
[25] origin and meaning cited on www.phrases.org.uk/meanings

to bring home a paycheck just as readily as I perceive the relationship between doing my homework and "making the grade." *A Snickers bar is a Snickers bar* whether it is used to motivate me to take action in an American-history class or in the kitchen. Those are just a few examples of how a person might prompt himself *or herself* to get up and get going in regard to fulfilling certain life's responsibilities.

What are some methods you can think of to spur yourself to arise and take action in fulfilling your own life's responsibilities?

_____

_____

_____

_____

_____

_____

_____

_____

_____

In considering some of your own observations and life experiences, what examples come to mind in which women have arisen early to make good use of time and energy in their lives and in their relationships with the men they knew? Those may include, but are not limited to, interactions between parents, grandparents, aunts and uncles, neighbors, and friends.

_____

_____

_____

_____

_____

_____

_____

_____

_____

How do you, as a woman, arise early to make good use of time and energy in your life and in your interactions with the men you know?

_____

_____

_____

_____

_____

_____

_____

_____

_____

In what ways do you perceive you might improve?

_____

_____

_____

_____

_____

_____

_____

_____

How might those improvements enhance your life and your relationships?

_____

_____

_____

_____

_____

_____

_____

_____

In sum, the womanly virtues enumerated by the author of Proverbs and further illustrated in this chapter include a woman's ability to develop trust in her relationship with a man and to perceive "that her merchandise *is* good" enough to willingly share her physical love with him. Also contained within that passage of scripture are a woman's desires to be anxiously engaged in life and to endeavor wholeheartedly in behalf of those whom she loves, to look unto the needs of others, and to speak words of wisdom and kindness to them. In addition, she directs her focus beyond sleep and idle pursuits in utilizing her time and energies, two of her most precious commodities, most wisely and effectively. Such characteristics are certainly worthy of emulation. What man would not want to follow that woman's lead in bettering himself that he might be found worthy to stand beside her? What man would not love her or look to caring for her needs, those of her children, and others whom she holds dear? In letting her "light so shine before men" (Matthew 5:16;[26] 3 Nephi 12:16),[27] woman wields great strength and power in the lives of her male counterparts, enough to change their existence, her own, and maybe even the course of history.

---

[26] *The Holy Bible.*
[27] *The Book of Mormon: Another Testament of Jesus Christ.*

Chapter Two

"If *She* Builds It,
He Will Come."[28]

A woman cannot be complete in a relationship with a man unless she is complete within herself. Thus, years of growth and preparation are required that she might offer herself as a worthy companion, one who can fully contribute to her union with the man whom she has chosen. The roles of womanhood are many and diverse. She is wife and mother, maker of her home, breadwinner in conjunction with her husband's income, avid learner, and one who explores and develops her own interests and abilities in many realms. Embarking upon marriage without having the basic building blocks necessary to engage in relationships, care for her home environment, earn a living, learn new things, and enjoy life is a dangerous undertaking and one from which many a woman may turn away in despair.

Marriage did not come quickly or easily to me. I was in my mid-thirties and 12 years my husband's senior when we met and fell in love. I had been a single mother for 14 years following a brief and disappointing marriage and prior to marrying once again. During that time, I had the opportunity to

----

[28] Gordon, L., & Gordon, C. (Producers), & Robinson, P. A. (Director). (1989). *Field of Dreams* [Motion Picture]. United States: Universal Studios.

strengthen and enhance those skills which perhaps I was lacking at the outset of my relationship history. I believe it was being put through the refiner's fire of single adulthood that brought me to the point of being a more livable and likable companion.

My Early Days

However, in describing my own journey towards personhood, I need to step back a bit further in time and to think of the early days in which I was unready to meet the challenges that lay ahead. For instance, in regard to relationships, though I was in my early twenties at the time of my first marriage, I had relatively little experience interacting with members of the opposite sex or of caring for children. Many women may have partaken of more dating or childcare opportunities at that age than I had. I, however, had thrown myself into scholastic endeavors to the exclusion of more practical matters in my pre-adult years and was entirely unprepared for what was about to happen. I met a man who wanted to marry me, and, though I was not entirely convinced that I loved him or wanted to marry him in return, I simply did not know how to say "no" or to trust my own instincts on that matter. As it was, I was drawn into a whirlwind courtship that culminated in marriage within not too many months and in pregnancy shortly thereafter. I found myself saddled to a man more "churlish" and abusive than Nabal, himself, and consider that brief *but monumental* episode in my life to be one of the most difficult learning experiences I have had the misfortune to undergo. I thought it would never end, but, thankfully, in time I learned that my extreme unhappiness would never bring joy either to myself or to my husband. I'd found that sacrificing one's own happiness for that of another is a complete misnomer as well as an absolute waste of time and energy. If one partner in a marriage is unhappy, so will the other be. Therefore, I found within myself the strength and courage to "abandon a sinking ship,"[29] and, while life as a single parent was not always easy or pleasure filled, at least the dangers were behind me and my little one.

Speaking of my daughter, as noted before, I had relatively little experience tending to the needs of children. Though I was raised with four younger siblings, my mother must not have imposed too much responsibility upon me for assistance with them, as having a child of my own took me by complete surprise. I had no idea what was involved in raising a child. I was scared to death of her. She wasn't like a doll that could be placed in her bed and forgotten about for hours on end. She needed my constant attention, and, despite my love for solitary endeavors, I knew I would never be alone again. That was a hard realization for me, and my daughter was a new learning experience, too, *but one I will never regret.* She has grown to be tall and beautiful, compassionate and intelligent, a leader among women, the strength of her home, and she has given me grandchildren I can also call my own. I think I'm finally grateful to know *I will never be alone again.*

In regard to caring for my household, though I have always been somewhat neat and orderly in approaching my home environment, I was known in the

---

[29] origin and meaning cited on www.phrases.org.uk/meanings

early days of my first marriage to leave dirty dishes in the sink and pots and pans on the stove for weeks at a time while away from home and visiting family. I remember returning from one such excursion to find that a pot full of grease had turned into a gelatinous mass and food-covered dishes were breeding life forms of their own. Believe me when I tell you it was quite the mess to clean up and not something a married woman can very well get away with if she wants to keep peace in her home. Spending weeks away from her household with her family of origin is also a questionable activity for one whose heart and hands should be devoted elsewhere. Even when her partner's away, army boot camp in that instance, the "mouse" really should not "play."[30]

As pertaining to earning an income, a woman in her early twenties often has not had the education or work experience necessary to procure a job that will meaningfully help to support her family. Such was the case with me. Though I had worked part-time jobs at a minimum-wage salary and even had occasion to hold down fulltime employment between academic quarters at my university, I was by no means capable of making a significant contribution to my family's financial wellbeing. I was on the right track in many respects. I had always treated my schooling seriously and upon marrying chose to pursue the degree which I was closest to completing. However, I had a long way to go. Jobs were not plentiful or lucrative in my field without at least finishing a master's program, and years of schooling lay ahead in that regard. That left me more dependent on an undependable man than I really

---

[30] origin and meaning cited on www.phrases.org.uk/meanings

cared to be. There was no safety in that. Due to a lack of preparation before marriage to meet the financial needs that would arise thereafter, my own and those of my daughter, I either had to remain in an intolerable marriage situation or had to return to a dependent position within my family of origin. Neither option seemed too pleasing. However, I chose plan B, the safer of the two paths, and went home to Mom and Dad.

In regard to learning new things and exploring and developing one's own interests and abilities, I believe I was a most adept pupil in my pre-marriage days. I loved to learn anything new and imagined myself capable of trying most anything that caught my fancy. One of the greatest joys of childhood is that we don't know our limitations or boundaries. We haven't run up against hard experience that has pushed us away or said "no" to our dreams and aspirations. Though I may not have been the most talented at everything I tried, I tried, nonetheless, and felt the better for it. I guess I would have to say that, of all the areas of marriage preparation under my current consideration, learning and trying new things was my forte. Dance and music, art and literature, sciences of all the hard and soft varieties were fair game to me. It was only upon marrying an injurious spouse that many of the stars began to fall from my eyes and I realized myself to be more contained than ever before. Then was the time to focus on practicality, on finding a way out of a difficult and precarious situation, and on staying in the safe zone.

A woman's journey towards becoming independent involves building a lifestyle in which she comes to treat and interact with family and friends in a characteristic way and in which her manner of living in her home environment can be transplanted from place to place. Also of great importance is the knowledge that she has fully invested herself in learning and experiencing those things necessary to procure a means of employment sufficient to sustain herself and her family. Another trait of mature womanhood is her continued desire to learn and to grow and to find joy and excitement in experiencing new things.

Though I am now only at middle adulthood and realize I have years ahead in which I may, yet, be seasoned by life, I can see the progression I have made since the early days of my unfortunate first marriage. As noted before, 14 years lay between the ending of one relationship through divorce and the culmination of another through a second marriage union, one that would bring far greater joy. I certainly did not lie stagnant during those years as a single woman with a child in tow, and mistakes were replete along the way as I have walked the path toward attaining greater maturity and ability to care for my life's responsibilities.

Dating relationships and friendships, too.

In regard to dating relationships, I have had more than a few of those since my early adulthood, enough to lend added insight into what I hoped to find in a union with my life's partner. Kindness and honor were among the attributes I most sought to encounter, as oftentimes, those qualities were sorely lacking in the men I knew, or at least the ones I entertained in my thoughts as romantic hopefuls. I did have some male friends in whom kindness and honor were not so absent, but my heart was not fully captivated in my associations with them, and there may have been other attributes that were wanting. In addition, a loyal and devoted approach to a partnership held great meaning for me, as again, I knew the sorrow of relating with those whose hearts belonged elsewhere. It was through gauging my response either to a lack or to a presence of a certain quality in a man that allowed me to weigh its relative importance in my life and in my quest for companionship. Therein, I was able to develop a picture of who would bring happiness to me versus who would not. Only then was I prepared to recognize him when he came along, and along he came when I was ready to perceive him.

My maternal grandmother also spoke of taking a good hard look at my grandfather's characteristics, in addition to leaning on her parents' perspective of him, in choosing him as her life's partner. They perceived him to be reliable, dependable, hard working, and kind, to be a good man, one who would bless my grandmother in enriching her life and freeing her from wants. Like Naomi of old had counseled with her daughter-in-law, Ruth, they, too, sought rest for my grandmother and that all should "be well with" her (Ruth 3:1).[31] Sound consideration on her own part and that of her parents certainly did not lead her astray on that account, and she and her offspring have benefited

---

[31] *The Holy Bible.*

immeasurably from Grandpa's frugal though generous approach to life even decades after his departure from it. Though Grandma also departed this life some years ago, those of us who remain are daily reminded of the bounteous legacy our grandfather left behind and why we love him still.

Grandpa displayed many admirable qualities despite some hardships he experienced in his youth. Though he received only an eighth-grade education due to his older brothers' being called away to fight in World War I and the necessity of his staying home to help his father run the family farm, he progressed in his later employment from being a salesman, to being a manager, to being the owner of a business establishment. A good work ethic born of earlier struggles served him well throughout his lifetime. In addition, he remained open to a life-long learning process and was obviously self-educated. For example, he could methodically solve the college accounting problems which stumped my mother and her classmates during her undergraduate program at a local university.

Getting back to the context of our discussion, in addition to dating relationships, friendships of both the same- and opposite-sex varieties are oftentimes fruitful places for considering characteristics that might be desirable in a marriage partner. As noted before, some of my male friends were not so lacking in admirable traits, and, over the years, I have had many relationships with men and women *both* in which the good and the bad in them *and in me* could be evaluated in creating a mental image of what I hoped to find in the man of my dreams as well as what I meant to avoid. I have also heard it said that fulltime missionaries, having dealt with multiple companions while serving their religious convictions, come away with a clearer understanding of whom they can live with and whom they can't. It's amazing to perceive the myriad of relationships which may lend insight to a woman's views of the man with whom she can abide "happily ever after."[32]

In regard to considering qualities that may be of value as a woman develops a picture of her perfect partner, she might benefit from looking to expert opinion on that matter. For instance, the creator of *eHarmony* has published numerous books on the subject, one of which I, myself, accessed not long before entering into my current marriage relationship.[33] The views of that author are not so different from those expressed by my own father, who suggested that creating a clear mental image of what one is looking for is essential to finding it. Not only does the author discuss the specifics of what to look for in finding a marriage partner, but he considers general factors that promote longevity and permanence in relationships as well. Such things as one's age at the time of marriage and the duration of one's courtship are among a variety of elements both considered and supported by research for their potential impact on one's wedded bliss.

In considering some of your own observations and life experiences, what examples of sound consideration (developing a clear understanding of what one is looking for) in women's relationships with men come to mind? Those may include, but are not limited to,

---

[32] origin and meaning cited on www.phrases.org.uk/meanings
[33] Warren, N. C. (1992). *Finding the Love of Your Life.* Colorado Springs, CO: Focus on the Family.

interactions between parents, grandparents, aunts and uncles, neighbors, and friends.

_____

_____

_____

_____

_____

_____

_____

_____

How do you, as a woman, employ sound consideration in your life and in your interactions with the men you know?

_____

_____

_____

_____

_____

_____

_____

_____

_____

In what ways do you perceive you might improve?

_____

_____

_____

_____

_____

_____

_____

_____

_____

How might those improvements enhance your life and your relationships?

_____

_____

_____

_____

_____

_____

_____

_____

_____

Parenting.

Fourteen years alone with a dependent child proved to be a veritable training ground in motherhood. Perhaps I shouldn't say that we were completely alone, as we spent some time living in homes with other family members and as my parents, grandmother, and siblings were often on hand to be of assistance, *sometimes of too much assistance*, but that is the price we pay for not being fully prepared when responsibility overtakes us. Nonetheless, my daughter, more than anyone, has trained me to be a parent. We have had our ups and downs, our good days and our bad. On the one hand, she has been known to be among the highest of scholastic performers and the most admirable of good citizens. On the other, she has risen to the heights of rebellion and thrown any form of propriety to the wind. For being one kid, she has experienced a lot of living, and, as her parent, whether fortunately, *or not so fortunately*, so have I. I believe I am a better parent today than I was at the outset of our relationship together. Not only have I had the world's best trainer, but, in addition, the job is unquestionably easier now that I have a partner standing beside me, one who is equally invested in the proper upbringing of my offspring.

I also believe I am a better grandparent than I was a parent. You know what they say about spoiling the grandkids and sending them home. It's "a piece of cake"[34] and "just deserts"[35] following years of "eating humble pie."[36] However, I also spent more quality time

[34] origin and meaning cited on www.phrases.org.uk/meanings
[35] origin and meaning cited on www.phrases.org.uk/meanings
[36] origin and meaning cited on www.phrases.org.uk/meanings

with my maternal grandmother than I did with my own mother during my upbringing and, therefore, may relate better with my grandchildren than I do at times with my own daughter. By way of explanation, my four younger siblings were considerably younger than my older brothers and I. They practically constituted a separate family from us and required a great deal of my parents' time and attention. Therefore, in regard to gaining the focus I was in need of as a young girl, my grandmother was the principal source of providing that for me as well as the primary example I would one day come to follow in teaching and interacting with my own posterity.

It is truly amazing how much one can learn about being a parent by being parented. Grandma's main concern upon my weekly arrival at her home was to see that I was fed, but she tended to my mental and emotional needs as well. She taught me about the things that she knew of, such as how to crack an egg without dropping shells in the bowl, how to bake a cake that would leave the consumer wanting more, how to wash both the front side *and the back side* of a dish, to prepare fruits and vegetables for canning, to daintily embroider a pillowcase, to crochet, to mend a sock with the use of a light bulb, and to launder clothing. I watched her as she perfectly removed the bones from a fish, cooked it in bacon grease, and served it with lemon. How savory that was! She also instructed me in the enjoyments of nature as, together, we inhaled the fragrant aromas of her vibrant flowerbeds and harvested the delicacies of her garden. We would sit for hours on her porch swing, watch the birds flittering in the trees, and listen to their songs. Beauty surrounded us in Grandma's tiny bit of paradise as cottonwoods towered upwards from the riverbank beyond. We could hear the sound of the river rushing by and the wind whispering through the trees and see the sun glinting between their verdant branches. Often, it was there that Grandma would tell me the stories of her childhood, of her life with Grandpa in their younger years, of her current dreams and hopes for herself and those whom she loved, and of fears and disappointments that time was still waiting to heal. Not just anyone was privileged to hear her speak that way, and I felt we had a special bond. There I learned to listen. There I learned to care. I loved to hear the sound of Grandma's voice and to feel the warmth of her hand on my back as she gently caressed me. For her, being a parent meant to teach, to spend time, to talk and to listen, to share all of life's sundry pleasures, and to give of her love. It meant caring for the basic needs of others and remembering her own lessons of life, which she readily imparted.

In addition to the parenting training I received from my maternal grandmother, in the aftermath of my divorce, my own parents "stepped up to the plate"[37] in overseeing my attempts to raise my daughter. I think that her birth was an awakening for them and a realization of the paucity of preparation I had undergone up to that point in learning how to nurture a child. They, therefore, parented me through my parenting. They hovered over me during my feeble attempts at breastfeeding a daughter who would literally have starved to death had it not been for the bottle, accompanied us to the doctor's office for checkups and immunizations, dropped my girl off at school and retrieved her once again in the early days of

---

[37] origin and meaning cited on www.phrases.org.uk/meanings

54

my graduate program, and sat with me through countless hours of tribulation while awaiting my daughter's return home after doing who knows what with who knows whom as a rebellious teenager. My parents kept me alive during my years as a single parent and before my husband's arrival onto the scene. I don't know what I would have done without them, and I don't envy any parent who has to go through it all alone. No one should have to endure the trials of parenthood without having someone else to lean on.

I realize my preparation as a parent is still in the making as the new generation appears on the horizon. However, I see how far I've come through the example and influence of some of the most important people in my life, those who have parented me, loved me, and looked to me to fulfill their needs. Having been strengthened by those relationships, I look to the future with hope I will continue to endure the challenges that may arise and to find joy and satisfaction in my posterity. In addition, there has been much written on parenting, and, while most parents would not consider themselves to be experts on the subject, those who do often readily share their views on such topics as discipline and dealing with emotional problems in children and adolescents. *Parent training*[38] on paying positive attention to children's good behaviors, offering effective commands, and making effective use of time

---

[38] Gimpel, G. A., & Holland, M. L. (2003). *Emotional and Behavioral Problems of Young Children: Effective Interventions in the Preschool and Kindergarten Years.* New York, NY: The Guilford Press.

out, *affective education*[39] for teaching children to understand and express their feelings, and *problem solving*[40] for assisting children to deal with life's everyday issues and concerns all play important roles in their proper nurturance and upbringing. The associated citations may prove beneficial not only for parents who find their situations to be especially challenging but also for those who are simply seeking to enhance the quality of their children's lives and of their own parent-child interactions.

In considering some of your own observations and life experiences, what examples of parenting training and preparation in women's lives come to mind? Those may include, but are not limited to, mothers, grandmothers, aunts, neighbors, and friends.

_____

_____

_____

_____

_____

_____

_____

_____

_____

[39] Merrell, K. W. (2001). *Helping Students Overcome Depression and Anxiety: A Practical Guide.* New York, NY: The Guilford Press.
[40] Kendall, P. C. (1992). *Stop and Think Workbook.* Merion Station, PA: P. C. Kendall.

As a woman, how do you employ, or how have you employed, parenting training and preparation in your life?

_____

_____

_____

_____

_____

_____

_____

_____

In what ways do you perceive you might improve?

_____

_____

_____

_____

_____

_____

_____

_____

How might those improvements enhance your life and your relationships?

_____

_____

_____

_____

_____

_____

_____

_____

Home environment.

Although my daughter and I spent considerable time living with family members following the demise of my first marriage, I was the maker of my own home for 11 years prior to marrying once again. That gave me the opportunity to clean and organize my surroundings relatively free of distraction and to explore the manner in which I wanted to live my home life. Furnishing my apartment when financial means came available was a form of self-expression. Comfort and beauty vied for being at the forefront of my attention. Comfortable couches and solid but stately tables occupied my common ground, and a bit of a country twist added flair to the dining area. Victorian wicker adorned my sleeping place, and floral paintings burst into life on every wall. Live plants and birds lent reality to the illusion. The artisan in me and the nature lover both were satisfied. I remember inviting a male friend home for dinner on one occasion and being greatly enlightened by a question he posed to me. Upon seeing the floral paintings hanging on the walls, the numerous plants inhabiting my dining-room table, and the sweet but cacophonous birds flittering in their cages, he asked, "You really like this kind of stuff?" That was all I needed to know *he was not the man for me*.

"If *you* build it, *he* will come," and all the ones that aren't right for you will scamper off in their own directions. A woman is looking for *the one* who can tolerate as well as love and appreciate her and *the one* whom she can stand to put up with as well. That's what marriage is all about. Those who set their sights on realistic and attainable outcomes are most likely to achieve them and to remain united with their partners with some degree of contentment over time. Whereas, others may lose interest in the relationship, and their focus may sooner or later shift elsewhere.

Tolerance is a key word here. According to Webster, *to tolerate* is "to bear without repugnance; to put up with; to suffer to be, or to be practiced or done, without prohibition or hindrance." A woman must learn to be who she is and "let the chips fall where they may."[41] She mustn't try to fit into someone else's mold of what he or she would make of her. She must learn who she is and come to understand what she wants her life to be and then put her insights into action. She must build the sort of lifestyle that she wants to live and attract the kind of people who will appreciate the things

---

[41] origin and meaning cited on www.phrases.org.uk/meanings

that she loves. Only then will *she* find *him, the one* who can tolerate, love, and appreciate her for being who she truly is when her reality speaks for itself.

In offering counsel and guidance for those who would seek to develop a unique lifestyle within their own home environments, I don't claim to be any Martha Stewart. However, Martha among others has provided timeless counsel on the subject, and many forms of media currently expound upon her ideas and the contributions of those who have followed in her footsteps. There is a book I have recently read that speaks of finding shelter from the storms of life within one's own home.[42] I believe I can suggest with some degree of confidence that those who are seeking to make of their homes "a haven in a hectic world" may turn to that book and find in large part what they are looking for.

"A haven in a hectic world" is a phrase most adequate to describe my maternal grandmother's home environment. A cool retreat from the summer's heat and a refuge from the winter's storm lay in wait for those who frequented her living space. Cleanliness and order abounded there. Sights and sounds were most entrancing, as Grandma loved to decorate and to find some means of entertaining others, if only through engaging them in some cheerful conversation. Tastes and smells were enticing, too, as Grandma loved to cook for others and as she did it so well. A particular childhood memory of mine is that of Grandma's old-fashioned popcorn popper, which invariably shed

---

[42] Moran, V. (1997). *Shelter for the Spirit: How to Make Your Home a Haven in a Hectic World.* New York, NY: HarperCollins Publishers, Inc.

plenty of excitement on evenings that may otherwise have been somewhat humdrum. She and I anxiously waited as the newly popped kernels pushed their way to the popper's brim and lifted its lid inches into the air. It was a rush to get the freshly popped corn poured safely into a bowl before it went cascading onto the floor. Pealed apple slices were a perfect compliment to our salty, buttery treat as we relaxed around Grandma's then state-of-the-art TV. Grandma was one who could take the peal off all in one long strand, yet another feat of sheer entertainment for a child.

Another memory from childhood illustrates the uniqueness of Grandma's decorating style, which could be seen in her tendency to take a yearly trip into the country with Grandpa to find the perfect tumbleweed. It was to be flocked, like a Christmas tree, and decorated with tiny lights and ornaments to adorn her home during the winter months. Around her beautifully displayed creation, Grandma would arrange her Christmas village, lighted from within, and, as children, we, her offspring, found a sense of joy and wonderment in gazing upon that magical scene. We each felt Grandma's love for us and knew we were favored in her eyes through the kindness and compassion which set the emotional tone of her household. Time and attention both were means of instilling her love, and the joy and wonderment we felt as children fill our hearts still as we envision through memory the days we spent at Grandma's house.

In considering some of your own observations and life experiences, what examples come to mind in which women have built a unique lifestyle within their home environments? Those may include, but are not limited to, mothers, grandmothers, aunts, neighbors, and friends.

_____

_____

_____

_____

_____

_____

_____

_____

_____

As a woman, how do you build, or how have you built, a unique lifestyle within your home environment?

_____

_____

_____

_____

_____

_____

_____

_____

_____

In what ways do you perceive you might improve?

_____

_____

_____

_____

_____

_____

_____

_____

_____

How might those improvements enhance your life and your relationships?

_____

_____

_____

_____

_____

_____

_____

_____

_____

Employment.

My journey toward self-sufficiency has been long and fraught with difficulty, and staying out of debt continues to be an ongoing struggle, even with a spouse to help sustain me in meeting the temporal needs of our family. However, I have devoted much time and attention to learning those things necessary to procure employment and to developing good work habits essential to maintain a job. As a single parent, I completed the remainder of a bachelor's program in my field of counseling and went on to receive a master's degree as well. After receiving my education, I found a job in a city an hour's journey from home, *the same city where my grandfather found his early employment.* I learned to drive a stick shift, as the car I fell in love with came equipped with standard transmission. I also had to overcome some inhibitions in traveling at highway speeds, as my prior excursions hadn't often taken me far from the valley where I was born, *my grandfather's birthplace also.* In addition, finding my way around a new city was somewhat of a challenge that had to be faced. However, I pushed past my fears and planted my roots into a new and exciting work experience. The job, itself, providing assessment and treatment services for clients at a public mental-health agency, was not such a "far cry"[43] from what I had done while in school, and I quickly settled into the routine. Not only was I well on my way toward becoming an independent woman of means, but I also espied a young man at my workplace, one whose admirable qualities soon won him a place in my heart *and shortly thereafter in my home.* Having gained fulltime employment with

[43] origin and meaning cited on www.phrases.org.uk/meanings

sufficient pay and benefits to sustain myself and my daughter, I was placed at an advantage, *like my grandfather before me*, to take steps in furthering other avenues of my life as well. *Marriage was soon forthcoming.*

Fulltime employment for both men *and women* is oftentimes necessary in forming partnerships in today's society. However, by no means is self-sufficiency for women a new or innovative idea thought of by our current generation. Women in past eras have not done things so differently from the way we do them today. My maternal grandmother, whom I have spoken of so highly, worked diligently throughout her childhood and young adulthood to earn the money necessary to meet her wants, while her parents provided for her needs. She picked produce on local farms, made candy in a confectionary, and even operated the elevator of a business building. In the early days of her marriage to my grandfather, she accompanied him on his excursions as a salesman for Pillsbury Mills through a nearby canyon into the communities which lay beyond. En route to their various destinations, she would crochet doilies to adorn her home, and, once having arrived, would treat her husband's customers to homemade pie crusts baked with Pillsbury flour and brimming with a cherry filling of which everyone who tasted it begged for more. She later labored beside my grandfather and their son in helping them to establish a family business, a farm-and-garden-supply store. She tended to the greenhouse, and everything she touched revealed her thumb to be golden. At various points in her life, she also raised and sold songbirds, chickens' eggs, and ferns from the flowerbeds which surrounded her home.

In addition, her mother, my maternal great-grandmother, was a woman of many means, whose merits, like those of the virtuous woman in Proverbs, "praise[d] her in the gates." Not having married until age 30, she was considered a "spinster" and of necessity had learned to support herself. She became a seamstress and a midwife, which endeavors endowed her with great ability to step into the role of wife and mother for a widower and his remaining five children following the deaths of several family members due to a bout of illness in the late 1800s. Her vocations, along with her abilities to work beside her husband on their farm and to cook well enough to be renowned throughout her community for her fine culinary skills, allowed her to care for a readymade family, nearly full grown, in addition to raising two sons and four daughters of her own.

As a point of interest, my maternal grandmother's parents had been pioneer children who each faced the death of a parent while crossing the sea or the plains. Hardships bred character and strength in them. Stories are replete of the mighty feats performed by my maternal great-grandfather, how he had served as a bodyguard for the second president of the Mormon Church, Brigham Young, how he had quarried rock for the building of the Salt Lake Temple, and how, while on one such excursion in the canyons surrounding the Salt Lake area, he had been attacked by a mountain lion and had killed it with a buggy whip. My maternal great-grandmother was also known in the area where she lived for her skill at delivering babies and having them neatly cleaned, dressed, and lying contentedly in their mothers' arms long before the doctor ever arrived. My favorite stories, however, are of the simple existence my great-grandparents led while supporting one another and, together, raising their family. I loved to hear of how my great-grandfather knew how to tell a "good" rabbit from a "bad" rabbit and how he would shoot and clean one and take it home to his wife, who would then stoke the fire and prepare all things necessary to bake a rabbit pie. I also love to remember the story of how my great-grandmother's butter was favored throughout their community over that made by any other because she put carrot juice in it to add extra flavor and color. The melons grown on their farm were also highly prized throughout their region.

Anyway, getting back to the idea of self-sufficiency for modern-day women, my mother always told me to "make hay while the sun shines."[44] It is better for a woman to learn to support her family before she has one to support than to face years of deprivation while endeavoring to correct deficits in employable skills after family responsibilities have already overtaken her. I can attest to that from personal experience and would hope that others might learn from the mistakes I have made not to follow in the footsteps of my early years. In doing so, any number of options might be considered as one seeks to attain the skills necessary to provide for oneself and one's family. Learning opportunities are most certainly available at any university. However, not everyone is destined for that sort of formal academic training, especially in light of financial and time constraints within which many people are forced to adapt. Just as meaningful might be a shorter and less costly involvement at a technical school or, better yet, an on-the-job apprenticeship that

---

[44] origin and meaning cited on www.phrases.org.uk/meanings

may lead to long-term employment in one's chosen field. The earlier one gets out the starting gate of employment, the more readily one might lend himself *or herself* to the responsibilities inherent in beginning a family life, which is, after all, the end goal for which each of us is striving in our work endeavors.

I have known of people whose opportunities for advanced education were thwarted very near the end of their degree programs and of others, who may have received their diplomas, who were unable to find or maintain employment in their chosen fields. Both conditions were seemingly beyond their control. While receiving an education for the sake of education, alone, is none other than a noble pursuit, it may be a luxury that comes at too high a price for one who seeks to contribute meaningfully to the financial wellbeing of his *or her* family. The time commitment, mental exertion, and monetary expenditure of such an undertaking may best be devoted directly to meeting the needs of those for whom one is immediately responsible.

In considering some of your own observations and life experiences, what examples of employment preparation in women's lives come to mind? Those may include, but are not limited to, mothers, grandmothers, aunts, neighbors, and friends.

_____

_____

_____

_____

_____

_____

_____

_____

_____

As a woman, how do you make use of, or how have you made use of, employment preparation in your life?

_____

_____

_____

_____

_____

_____

_____

_____

In what ways do you perceive you might improve?

_____

_____

_____

_____

_____

_____

_____

_____

_____

How might those improvements enhance your life and your relationships?

_____

_____

_____

_____

_____

_____

_____

_____

Forever learning and trying new things.

As I mentioned previously, I had been a most astute pupil of life prior to my first marriage and the hardships that unfortunately accompanied it and had found my strength in learning and trying new things. If I had to evaluate my areas of strength today, they would probably be *anything and everything but learning and trying new things.* I think that's because my life as a woman is overrun with responsibilities. I am a wife, a mother, a grandmother, an employee, and a maker of my home. With all the duties of life pressing so heavily upon me, it is all but impossible to find the time and energy necessary to expand my mind or to explore my interests. I catch myself looking to the distant future with some degree of envy and thoughts that I may one day feel free to learn and to grow once again as I did in my childhood. Maybe that's what retirement's all about. At least, I hope so. In any regard and by whatever means it comes about, being someone and something of value and importance in the life of another depends greatly on our willingness to learn and to try new things. How else can we show our interest in those whom we love? How else can we adapt to the changes our relationships with them naturally bring into our lives?

I vividly recall my first excursion out and about with the man I now call my husband. It wasn't my first trip to the west desert of northwestern Utah and southwestern Idaho. It was my second, to be exact. The first outing had been taken with my family of origin when I was but a child, and the desert heat and barrenness of the landscape were none too pleasing to me, so little that I failed to make the journey once again until someone young and handsome offered to take me along as his sole companion. I figured *there would at least be something pleasant to look at* and didn't mind the idea of being the primary focus of his attention as well. As it was, there was vast beauty all around us that completely defies my ability to describe it. The difference between my first impression of the west desert and my second, *more favorable* reaction to it was that *I* had to look through *his* eyes to see things in a way I had never seen them before. That's the kind of learning and trying new things I think is of greatest value and importance in relationships. *She* learns something of what *he* knows. *He* tries something because *she* loves it.

I remember glancing through a book about deep-sea fishing.[45] My sister had checked it out for me at a local library and had encouraged me to read it as a means of preparing for my upcoming marriage. Anyone may naturally wonder what in the world deep-sea fishing has to do with marriage. In regard to the book in question, it had everything to do with marriage. It was written by a woman about the man she loved and about the avocation he adored. His primary interest became a fascination for her as well, as she channeled a willingness to learn and experiment upon new things in a direction that would naturally strengthen her bond with him. There's a great deal of truth in the notion that *a woman can catch a man by watching him catch a fish.*

Every man, like every woman, is unique in the things that he loves. Some men like kicking about in the sticks of the vast open territory of the west desert. My father was one of those. Others like to fish. My lineage is replete with fishermen as well. Whether it be sports or other recreational activities, foods and entertainments, personal haunts and lifelong friendships, vocations and avocations alike, it is not unwise for a woman to develop and display an interest in the most treasured pursuits of the man who adores her. He can only cherish her more as she shows forth a willingness to adapt to his lifestyle while sharing with him some interests of her own.

---

[45] I don't remember the author or the title of the book.

In offering guidance on how to go about doing that, I might suggest that *she* select a passive approach in allowing *him* to take the lead in suggesting and implementing plans for the time they will spend together. It is through a patient and self-sacrificing mode that she will learn the most about him, of "his tastes, his passions, his pursuits,"[46] and through her observations as his frequent companion that she will discern those things which most please him. Her added insight in that regard cannot but strengthen their union should she chose him as her life's partner, at which time she, too, may begin to share some interests of her own.

In considering some of your own observations and life experiences, what examples of learning and trying new things in women's relationships with men come to mind? Those may include, but are not limited to, interactions between parents, grandparents, aunts and uncles, neighbors, and friends.

_____

_____

_____

_____

_____

_____

_____

---

[46] Doran, L. (Producer), & Lee, A. (Director). (1995). *Sense and Sensibility* [Motion Picture]. United Kingdom: Columbia Pictures.

_____

_____

How do you, as a woman, employ learning and trying new things in your life and in your interactions with the men you know?

_____

_____

_____

_____

_____

_____

_____

_____

In what ways do you perceive you might improve?

_____

_____

_____

_____

_____

_____

_____

How might those improvements enhance your life and your relationships?

_____

_____

_____

_____

_____

_____

_____

_____

The scriptures recount the parable of the ten virgins (Matthew 25:1-13),[47] in which five of them, having trimmed their lamps with oil, were prepared for the arrival of the bridegroom and to enter into the marriage feast. The other five, however, were dismally unprepared for events that were to overtake them. They went searching for oil, and, in their absence, the bridegroom came, and went, and shut the door behind him. I liken my lack of preparation for my first marriage to the foolish virgins, who, wanting oil, had failed to make ready all things necessary to take on the added responsibilities associated with mature

[47] _The Holy Bible._

75

womanhood.   Doors of opportunity quickly closed before me as I gazed upon my empty lamp. Fortunately, I consider my degree of readiness for my second marriage to have been far more comparable to that of the wise virgins, whose alacrity and well-trimmed lamps allowed them entrance through the door. Becoming a life's partner, caring for my children and my home, etching out my place in the world through vocational endeavors and pursuit of avocations all required my diligent effort and careful use of time. Yet, those years of preparation through concentrated exertion were required to gain entrance through a door which had been closed to me before.   No degree of regret or last-minute attempt to overcome vast deficits on my part could ever replace being truly prepared when the bridegroom finally came.

Chapter Three
Her Place beside Him

In coming to understand her place beside the man whom she has chosen, a woman can learn much from studying the generations of women who have gone before her. *Is it possible to see the future without looking into the past?* I think not in regard to a woman's relationship with a man. One couple is not truly unique from another pertaining to the basic elements that breed for a happy existence between husband and wife. God, Himself, deemed that it was "not good" for man to be alone in the Garden of Eden. Therefore, He prepared woman to be "an help meet for" man (Genesis 2:18;[48] Moses 3:18;[49] Abraham 5:14).[50] According to Webster, *to help* is "to provide assistance to; to contribute aid to; to cooperate with; to succor, to relieve; to remedy; to benefit; to promote; to be of use to; to facilitate." To be *meet* is to be "fit; suitable; proper; appropriate." Thus, according to scriptural account, the purpose of woman's creation was to enhance the existence of man through their well-appointed partnership, and that she has done from the beginning of time. Would Adam have ventured forth from the protective realm of the garden had Eve not encouraged him?

---

[48] *The Holy Bible.*

[49] Corporation of the President of the Church of Jesus Christ of Latter-Day Saints. (1981). *The Pearl of Great Price.* Salt Lake City, UT: The Church of Jesus Christ of Latter-Day Saints.

[50] *The Pearl of Great Price.*

Through the scriptures, women are counseled to "*be* in subjection to [their] own husbands" and to adorn themselves with "a meek and quiet spirit, which is in the sight of God of great price" (1 Peter 3:1, 4).[51]

For after this manner in the old time the holy women also, who trusted in God, adorned themselves, being in subjection unto their own husbands: Even as Sara obeyed Abraham, calling him lord: whose daughters ye are, as long as ye do well, and are not afraid with any amazement (1 Peter 3:5, 6).[52]

Thus, a woman's relationship with God comes into play in her interrelatedness with man. She must trust in *His* holy order, or expect with some degree of confidence that being placed in subjection to a man will do her "good and not evil all the days of her life," as noted in Proverbs. God has counseled man to "dwell with [woman] according to knowledge, giving honour unto the wife, as unto the weaker vessel, and as being heirs together of the grace of life; that [their] prayers be not hindered" (1 Peter 3:7).[53] It appears that being united as a couple places a man and a woman in a special relationship with God to which they cannot attain separately and which must follow His holy order if they are to please Him and fully benefit from their relationship with one another. Such goes beyond my ability to fully comprehend, but can I allow myself to trust in *Him* enough to put *His* prescription to the test? That is a question which each woman must ask herself as she contemplates engaging in a union with a man.

---

[51] *The Holy Bible.*
[52] *The Holy Bible.*
[53] *The Holy Bible.*

Nowhere is found a greater example of woman's trust in God than Mary, the mother of Christ, who, when approached by the angel, Gabriel, and told that she would conceive a son by the power of the Holy Ghost, meekly replied, "Behold the handmaid of the Lord; be it unto me according to thy word" (Luke 1:38).[54] Who among women would be as trusting when asked to subject herself to a man?

What does it mean for a woman to be in subjection to a man? Webster indicates that *a subject* is "one who is under the dominion or rule of a sovereign, esp. one who owes allegiance to a government and who lives under its protection; one who or that which is under the control or influence of another." *Being subject* is "being under dominion, rule, or authority, as of a monarch, state, or some governing power; owing allegiance or obedience to a supreme authority; being under domination, control, or influence." *To subject* is "to bring under dominion, rule, or authority, as of a governing power," to "bring under dominion, control, or influence." By way of example, one might consider the planets, which, themselves, are under the control or influence of other planets. Through the scriptures, we read that "Kolob is after the reckoning of the Lord's time" and "is set nigh unto the throne of God, to govern all those planets which belong to the same order as that upon which [we] stand" (Abraham 3:9).[55] Such is also the case with people, between men and women in particular. Throughout history and inherent in every society there has been an imposition of one man's rule or authority over another. Depending on the sovereign

---

[54] *The Holy Bible.*
[55] *The Pearl of Great Price.*

79

in question, he *or she* has either benefited or harmed those held in subjection to his *or her* dominion. Man, however, in his relationship with woman, may claim a more natural versus imposed sovereignty. He is, as God, *Himself*, a man and closer to the throne of God due to the similarity of his composition. He is, therefore, set next to God in holding authority over woman. Depending on the man, his dominion may either benefit or harm her. Does woman have a choice in being ruled by man? I think not, as that is the natural order of things, but she does have a choice as to whom she selects as her lord and master or if she elects to have one at all.

Based upon the opportunities that come her way, every woman has the freedom to choose for herself what she will be, either married, whether happily or unhappily so, or single. My choice was to terminate an unhappy marriage many years ago and to abide singly for some time until fortune smiled upon me with a far greater opportunity for happiness. My choice today is whether or not to heed the counsel of my husband. I know his expectations of me, and I believe I know what God intends as well. "Mine house is a house of order, saith the Lord God, and not a house of confusion" (D&C 132:8).[56] "No [household] can serve two masters: for either [they] will hate the one, and love the other; or else [they] will hold to the one, and despise the other" (Matthew 6: 24).[57] I believe that is where our world society in general and our country in particular have strayed in regard to the covenants a man and a woman make at the time of marriage. In former years,

---

[56] *The Doctrine and Covenants of the Church of Jesus Christ of Latter-Day Saints.*
[57] *The Holy Bible.*

a woman knew of her place in relation to that of a man. By choosing him as her marriage partner and allowing him to choose her, she then willingly submitted to his counsel and guidance in overseeing the course of their lives together. If her husband happened to be of a wise and benevolent nature, it was so much the better for her to be directed by him. In the scriptures, we read,

> If it were possible that you could have just men to be your kings, who would establish the laws of God, and judge this people according to his commandments, yea, if ye could have men for your kings who would do even as my father Benjamin did for this people—I say unto you, if this could always be the case then it would be expedient that ye should always have kings to rule over you (Mosiah 29:13).[58]

Such is also the case in a marriage situation. However, it is also important to consider the destructive force an evil and wicked man can have in the lives of those who are held subject to him. In the scriptures, we also read,

> Now I say unto you, that because all men are not just it is not expedient that ye should have a king or kings to rule over you. For behold, how much iniquity doth one wicked king cause to be committed, yea, and what great destruction! Yea, remember king Noah, his wickedness and his abominations, and also the wickedness and abominations of his people. Behold what great destruction did come upon them; and also because

---

[58] *The Book of Mormon: Another Testament of Jesus Christ.*

81

of their iniquities they were brought into bondage (Mosiah 29:16-18).[59]

In former years, a woman who knew of her place in relation to that of a man likely had greater stability in her marriage union, as she knew what to expect and how to proceed in her interactions with her husband. If she had chosen her partner well, she likely benefited from abiding by the natural order set before her. If she had failed to make a wise decision, the great potential was that she suffered. Nonetheless, her marriage likely endured through both her own and society's expectations of her partnership. In modern times, however, priorities have shifted. Women are uncertain as to where they belong in the world of men and may attempt to override the rules that for generations have provided structure encompassing the interactions between men and women in genteel society. A constant struggle for the role of leadership has replaced the peace and contentment that abided in the status quo. The institutions of marriage and family have been placed at risk as self-focus has taken precedence over a concern for the welfare of others.

If a woman cannot exercise wisdom in choosing the man with whom she will spend her life or abide within the dictates of his counsel, perhaps she should abide alone. However, if she is one upon whom fortune has smiled in receiving a good husband and can bend enough to subject herself to his benevolent will, there are a few things she should keep in mind as she embarks upon a journey that may last a lifetime. Following are some humble *but meaningful* suggestions

---

[59] *The Book of Mormon: Another Testament of Jesus Christ.*

that are intentioned to enhance her experience and to enrich her understanding as to where *she* fits in *his* world and how she can contribute to their mutual satisfaction as husband and wife.

Let Him Shine.

The Lord's counsel to Emma Smith, wife of Joseph Smith, Jun., the first prophet, seer, and revelator of the Church of Jesus Christ of Latter-Day Saints, in addition to other instructions given to her pertaining to her callings in her mortal ministry, was to "continue in the spirit of meekness, and beware of pride. Let thy soul delight in thy husband, and the glory which shall come upon him" (D&C 25:14).[60] "And verily, verily, I say unto you, that this is my voice unto all. Amen" (D&C 25:16).[61] According to Webster, to be *meek* is to be "mild of temper; gentle; not easily provoked or irritated; submissive." He defines *pride* as "the quality or state of being proud; an unreasonable opinion of one's own superiority over others; inordinate self-esteem; the reflection of this quality in disdainful or arrogant behavior." To be *prideful* is to be "full of pride; haughty; arrogant; insolent." Emma was encouraged to be meek and to refrain from pride in giving her husband center stage and allowing him to shine in his own specific realm. All other women are encouraged to do likewise in regard to their relationships with their husbands.

---

[60] *The Doctrine and Covenants of the Church of Jesus Christ of Latter-Day Saints.*
[61] *The Doctrine and Covenants of the Church of Jesus Christ of Latter-Day Saints.*

Of what benefit might that be to a woman? Most obviously, replacement of self-focus with focus on others enlarges her capacity to love and to extend herself in the giving of service. Such focus and attention given with enthusiasm is truly one of the greatest gifts a woman can offer a man. Children certainly seek their parents' positive focus as a means of gaining self-esteem, and men and women both may carry similar needs well into their adult relationships. Enhancing a man's self-esteem by offering him a positive focus of her attention is one means by which a woman can endear him to her and breed a sense of loyalty in their union just as children gain a sense of loyalty and devotion to caring parent figures.

King David, who, as discussed in a previous chapter, was honored in his fortuitous interactions with Abigail, was dishonored in an interchange with another wife, Michal, the daughter of Saul, David's mortal enemy and the king whom he succeeded to the throne. David, in his rejoicing at bringing the ark of God into the city of Jerusalem, leapt and danced before the Lord and the people of the city while somewhat scantily clad in a linen ephod. Michal, having espied his behavior through a window, "despised him in her heart" (2 Samuel 6:16)[62] and sought to shame him for his actions. Upon David's return home, Michal spoke words of bitterness to him when, instead, she might have shared in his delight. David's sense of betrayal brought a sudden end to their physical union, and Michal remained childless throughout the remainder of her life (2 Samuel 6:12-23).[63] What a great price to pay for

---

[62] *The Holy Bible.*
[63] *The Holy Bible.*

84

injuring another's pride, which, according to Webster, can also mean "a reasonable self-respect based on a consciousness of worth." Michal's disrespect was intentioned to shame David and to engender a sense of unworthiness in him. Upon succeeding in her goal, she lost many of the blessings associated with the "meek and quiet spirit, which is in the sight of God of great price" (1 Peter 3:4).[64] The scriptures counsel that "only by pride cometh contention" (Proverbs 13:10)[65] and that "pride *goeth* before destruction, and an haughty spirit before a fall" (Proverbs 16:18).[66] Michal's pride was a destructive force in her marriage and caused her to fall from the good graces of her husband.

If a woman's goal is to be the beloved focus of her "knight in shining armor,"[67] she must allow him to shine and not dampen his spirit of enjoyment in all else that he holds dear. By so doing, she enhances his sense of self-worth, which is so important in motivating *him* to take action in *her* behalf as she stands in need of his assistance. "What comes around [definitely] goes around"[68] in the circle of love she can engender through her acceptance and appreciation of his many fine qualities, which won him her heart in the first place. Once again, taking a passive, or meek, approach while being patient and self-sacrificing in refraining from pride are attributes necessary in offering *him* center stage, or the full focus of *her* attentions.

---

[64] *The Holy Bible.*
[65] *The Holy Bible.*
[66] *The Holy Bible.*
[67] origin and meaning cited on www.phrases.org.uk/meanings
[68] origin and meaning cited on www.phrases.org.uk/meanings

In considering some of your own observations and life experiences, what examples come to mind in which "a meek and quiet" versus prideful spirit in women allowed them to delight in their husbands, to let them shine, and to avoid the contentions that may otherwise have been forthcoming? Those may include, but are not limited to, interactions between parents, grandparents, aunts and uncles, neighbors, and friends.

_____

_____

_____

_____

_____

_____

_____

_____

How do you, as a woman, employ "a meek and quiet" versus prideful spirit in your life and in your interactions with the men you know?

_____

_____

_____

_____

_____

_____

_____

_____

_____

In what ways do you perceive you might improve?

_____

_____

_____

_____

_____

_____

_____

_____

*How might those improvements enhance your life and
your relationships?*

_____

_____

_____

_____

_____

_____

Heed His Counsel.

> Wives, submit yourselves unto your own husbands,
> as unto the Lord. For the husband is the head of
> the wife, even as Christ is the head of the church:
> and he is the saviour of the body. Therefore as the
> church is subject unto Christ, so _let_ the wives _be_ to
> their own husbands in every thing (Ephesians 5:22-
> 24).[69]

According to Webster, _to submit_ is "to yield to the
decision or opinion of another" in a state of "surrender,
compliance, or obedience." The scriptures counsel
women to yield to the opinions and decisions of their
husbands. Husbands are counseled "to love their wives
as their own bodies" (Ephesians 5:28)[70] and wives to
reverence their husbands (Ephesians 5:33).[71]
Reverence is "an attitude of deep respect and esteem
mingled with affection; veneration; an obeisance or
respectful act." The scriptures aren't necessarily
instructing women to pay obeisance to their husbands
but to hold them in _esteem_, or high regard, respect,
admiration, or favor, to regard them "as having a
certain value; as, to _esteem_ his opinions valuable."

---

[69] _The Holy Bible._
[70] _The Holy Bible._
[71] _The Holy Bible._

To counsel is "to advise or give deliberate opinion; to exhort, warn, admonish, or instruct; to recommend." According to the scriptures, "Where no counsel *is*, the people fall: but in the multitude of counsellors *there is* safety" (Proverbs 11:14).[72]   In addition, "Without counsel purposes are disappointed: but in the multitude of counsellors they are established" (Proverbs 15:22).[73] Finally, "*Every* purpose is established by counsel" (Proverbs 20:18).[74]   We are told, "The virtuous, shall seek counsel" (D&C 122:2).[75]   As discussed in a previous chapter, *virtue* is an "inherent power to produce effects; potency." *Purpose* is synonymous with intent and *effect* with result. A virtuous woman will bring her purposes, or intentions, to fruition, effect, or result by seeking the counsel of her husband or other male figure holding some authority over her.

As a woman living singly for many years of my life, I sought the counsel of my father and held him in esteem as one who could instruct me based on the wisdom and experience of his greater years. I also held in high regard the instruction of a religious and secular advisor in the field of counseling, a man who was a contemporary of my father. I looked to the advice of those male figures in all aspects of my life, including parenting, schooling, work endeavors, and relationships. It has been some years since I have heard either voice echoing in my ears, as both have passed beyond the veil and my ability to hear them, and I miss the solid counsel of their words.

---

[72] *The Holy Bible.*

[73] *The Holy Bible.*

[74] *The Holy Bible.*

[75] *The Doctrine and Covenants of the Church of Jesus Christ of Latter-Day Saints.*

I now seek the advisement of one far younger and less experienced in the ways of the world but equipped, nonetheless, in guiding my purposes to safe harbor. He is the man I married almost a decade ago and who has grown with me in becoming a life's companion and in accepting his role as teacher and advisor in my life. I now look to him as being *the one* who can calm the troubled storms of my existence and bolster and encourage me to continue on my life's journey. I think I would be lost without him. I know I would be lacking much. I look to him on a daily basis for comfort and direction in my roles as wife and mother, maker of my home, one who works for a living and who also seeks satisfaction through avocations. I am writing this book at his suggestion and benefiting immeasurably thereby. I didn't realize before I undertook this endeavor how gratifying it would be to put pen to paper, *or fingertips to computer keyboard, in my case*, in documenting my thoughts and sharing them with an imaginary multitude. It makes me feel important, like someone really wants to hear what I have to say. It calms me and nourishes my soul to think higher thoughts than the mundane imaginations of my ordinary existence. Herein, I have found peace.

I've put my husband's suggestion to the test and found it to be good. Therein, I've come to value his opinion. Can other women do the same? I believe they can in regard to their relationships with their own husbands. It isn't so difficult if they'll merely give it a try. A woman must have faith enough to try (Alma 32:28-43),[76] hope in things unseen (Hebrews 11;[77]

---

[76] *The Book of Mormon: Another Testament of Jesus Christ.*
[77] *The Holy Bible.*

Alma 32:21;[78] Ether 12:6),[79] if she is to realize the blessings that come from submitting herself to the counsel of her husband. The scriptures are replete with examples of what comes from putting faith to the test, but does a woman love her husband enough to have faith in him and the wisdom of his words? Perhaps, by putting his counsel to the test, she will learn to love him even more.

I've also found that the best way to seek my husband's counsel is simply to ask for it. Seldom does a day go by without my feeling some degree of anxiety or depression about the sundry nagging influences outside my immediate home environment. I'm certain that any woman with varied contacts or work responsibilities apart from home can sympathize. It's hard to focus my full attentions on my family and my household without being able to unload a bit of the burden which I invariably hold within. It is during times of greatest stress that I share those concerns with my husband and request his feedback on how best to approach my dilemmas in ameliorating their detrimental effects on my life. A man may feel that he needs to fix things or that, if he fails to offer a sound and immediate solution, he is failing a woman somehow. However, it is simply my husband's efforts to understand and appreciate my situation for being the unique combination of circumstances that it is and his attempts to convey his support and desire to be of assistance that truly mean the most to me. As I express my gratitude to him for the help he offers and attempt

[78] *The Book of Mormon: Another Testament of Jesus Christ.*
[79] *The Book of Mormon: Another Testament of Jesus Christ.*

to follow his advice, I am hopefully ensuring his continued counsel in days to come.

In considering some of your own observations and life experiences, what examples come to mind in which women have heeded the counsel of their husbands and, by so doing, benefited? Those may include, but are not limited to, interactions between parents, grandparents, aunts and uncles, neighbors, and friends.

_____

_____

_____

_____

_____

_____

_____

_____

_____

_____

How have you, as a woman, heeded the counsel of the important men in your life and, by so doing, benefited?

_____

_____

_____

_____

_____

_____

_____

_____

_____

In what ways do you perceive you might improve?

_____

_____

_____

_____

_____

_____

_____

_____

_____

How might those improvements enhance your life and your relationships?

_____

_____

_____

_____

_____

_____

_____

_____

_____

Comfort Him.

Emma Smith was counseled that "the office of [her] calling [was to] be for a comfort unto [the Lord's] servant, Joseph Smith, Jun., [her] husband, in his afflictions, with consoling words, in the spirit of meekness" (D&C 25:5).[80] Webster's definition of *comfort* is "to raise from depression; to sooth when in grief or trouble; to bring solace or consolation to; to console, to cheer; to hearten; to solace; to enliven." To *console* is "to cheer, as a person, in distress or depression; to comfort; to sooth; to solace." Not every man is as afflicted with troubles as was the Lord's prophet, Joseph Smith, Jun., nor given as great responsibilities to carry as were placed upon him, and Emma's calling to comfort and console him was a weighty one. However, every man, woman, and child is in need of consolation from time to time, and one of the greatest callings of womanhood, of wives and mothers in particular, is to offer the solace that is needed in times of hardship and despair.

My maternal grandmother was a great one to bring comfort into the lives of those whom she loved. As a child and young woman, I was a frequent recipient of her tender care and words of encouragement. Her whole life was devoted to strengthening and uplifting

[80] *The Doctrine and Covenants of the Church of Jesus Christ of Latter-Day Saints.*

the members of her family, and she fulfilled her mission well into the tenth decade or her mortal existence. Her husband, my grandfather, was a primary focus of her loving attentions, and, despite having had some serious physical-health problems throughout his life, he managed to live well into his ninth decade. Grandma was meticulous in ensuring that his nutritional needs were met, as medical treatments for severe ulcerations had left him with only a third of his stomach capacity to aid his digestion. She also nursed him through a frightening bout of blood poisoning that almost cost him his arm and perhaps even his life. Beyond the physical care she offered was the calm and loving assurance that all would be well and that no challenge was too great to face as long as she was standing beside him *or any of us who were fortunate enough to be blessed by her love.*

The scriptures counsel us to "succor the weak, lift up the hands which hang down, and strengthen the feeble knees" (D&C 81:5;[81] Isaiah 35:3;[82] Hebrews 12:12).[83] That is such an important aspect of being a woman in a relationship with a man. There are many facets of a man's life which can penetrate his inner fortress and bring him to his knees. Men in particular have been burdened with the responsibility to care for the temporal wellbeing of their families and to provide for their physical needs. Thus, employment, either in or out of the home, has been considered a necessity as long as man has abided on the earth. Caring for oneself is oftentimes obligation enough, let alone having to

[81] *The Doctrine and Covenants of the Church of Jesus Christ of Latter-Day Saints.*
[82] *The Holy Bible.*
[83] *The Holy Bible.*

bear up under the added responsibility of a family. Thus, the stress level of a married man may be relatively high compared to that of someone with a lesser burden to bear. At the end of his workday, all *he* wants is to be nurtured by *her*, to be loved and cared for, to be appreciated for his efforts and acknowledged for his attempts to make a positive difference in her life. Thus, it is truly as important for her to be as sweet and cheerful in her interactions with him as it was for all her female forebears in the generations which have gone before. A woman truly does set the emotional tone of her household. Many a woman may lament that statement as being all too Fifties. I hail the Fifties as being a time of selfless love and the women of that generation as setting a shining example of what it means to be a woman in a relationship with a man.

I remember times of sadness and despair in my own life in which I was in need of comfort and consolation. A disappointed relationship was soothed by a family pet which tirelessly clung to its position on my lap and refused to be displaced until a portion of my anguish had dispersed. A young grandchild sat beside me and expressed her love as I struggled with inner turmoil over how to resolve the financial concerns which beset me. Youth and innocence are oftentimes equated with the meekness and gentleness that are required to quietly, patiently allow others to feel their pain and to come to some sort of internal resolution, aided by a calming presence. To be "as [a] little child" (Matthew 18:4)[84] is a great blessing in the lives of those who seek a calming presence and the assurance that all will be well. King Solomon, himself, was not above

---

[84] *The Holy Bible.*

admitting to the Lord, "I *am but* a little child" (1 Kings 3:7).[85] Far be it for any of us to strive to be more or less than that in comforting those whom we love.

In addition, a woman's touch can be the salve, or "balm in Gilead" (Jeremiah 8:22),[86] in the lives of those who love her. Hers is a healing touch and necessary in assuring others of her love. Memories of my grandmother's gentle caress of my back as a young child still sustain me in facing life's difficulties, especially those which bring physical pain, and encourage me to offer similar comforts to those for whom I am responsible to provide care. The child whom my daughter was expecting in chapter one is now newly born and entirely entranced by the gentle touches intended to lessen his discomforts in life. Little children love the comfort of touch, but what man or woman would shun the offer of a backrub or a foot massage from his or her partner after a long day's labor? He or she would be the exception to the rule, and *the rule should always be to offer and accept the comforts afforded through the gentle touch of one who cares.*

So, in offering the comfort a man stands in need of as he looks to fulfill the responsibilities that have been set before him, a woman can provide words of consolation, her calm and assuring presence, and a kind and gentle touch. Such go far toward fulfilling her responsibilities as the primary caregiver in her home and the source of strength and support for the ones she loves.

---

[85] *The Holy Bible.*
[86] *The Holy Bible.*

In considering some of your own observations and life experiences, what examples come to mind in which women have offered comfort to the men in their lives? Those may include, but are not limited to, interactions between parents, grandparents, aunts and uncles, neighbors, and friends.

_____

_____

_____

_____

_____

_____

_____

_____

_____

How do you, as a woman, offer comfort to the men in your life?

_____

_____

_____

_____

_____

_____

_____

_____

_____

In what ways do you perceive you might improve?

_____

_____

_____

_____

_____

_____

_____

_____

_____

How might those improvements enhance your life and your relationships?

_____

_____

_____

_____

_____

_____

_____

Be Prudent.

The scriptures teach us that "a prudent wife *is* from the Lord" (Proverbs 19:14).[87] What does it mean to be prudent? *To be prudent* is to be "judicious and cautious in managing practical affairs; circumspect; sagacious; shrewd in planning for the future; provident; characterized or directed by prudence, as an action." *Prudence* is "the quality or fact of being prudent; cautious, practical wisdom; good judgment; discretion; provident care in management; economy or frugality" (Webster, of course). The scriptures instruct women on prudential living. Timothy counseled "the younger women [to] marry, bear children, guide the house, [and] give none occasion to the adversary to speak reproachfully" (1 Timothy 5:14).[88] Titus encouraged "the young women to be sober, to love their husbands, to love their children, *To be* discreet, chaste, keepers at home, good, obedient to their own husbands, that the word of God be not blasphemed" (Titus 2:4-5).[89] A virtue among women, as enumerated by the author of Proverbs, is that "she looketh well to the ways of her household."

Finances are often of great concern to individuals and couples alike and may be the source of much contention between husbands and wives if financial means are not properly allocated to meet the needs of

---

[87] *The Holy Bible.*

[88] *The Holy Bible.*

[89] *The Holy Bible.*

all involved. That is why economy and frugality are such an important part of prudential living. My maternal grandfather once told my grandmother that he could not have imagined being able to support any other woman as his wife due to my grandmother's wise and careful use of their financial resource, especially in times of economic hardship. Both of my maternal grandparents were born of pioneer ancestry, and both knew the meaning of hard work in procuring the means necessary to meet their own personal needs prior to marriage. Perhaps that is why similar care was taken to preserve their limited financial resource after the advent of their marriage and while raising a family during the economic devastation of the Great Depression. My mother mentioned what a blessing it was not to suffer financially, as so many others did during that time, due to her parents' wisdom in earning and allocating their resource.

Not all women are as fortunate, *or unfortunate, depending on how one may perceive her situation,* as my grandmother was to be blessed with the hardships that she knew in her early years. Therefore, not all women may be as well versed in the fine arts of economy and frugality as was she. However, use of wisdom in allocating financial resource is a skill that can be learned, and every woman might benefit from availing herself of the opportunity to gain such knowledge. I learned through a brief tutorial once how to go about developing a budget for my finances. I may not always follow the instruction I was given but can see where it would be to my advantage if I were to do so.

Developing a budget is a step-by-step process that involves looking at and evaluating present expenditures as well as allocating finite resources to meet future needs. First, one must record all expenditures over a given period of time, for instance, a month, or a 3-month quarter if not all expenses, such as insurance premiums, come due on a monthly basis. That can easily be done by keeping a notebook and writing utensil readily available at all times to record the date, type, and amount of each disbursement. Next, one must categorize each expense to see how much resource is being allocated to given wants and needs over time. Categorizing expenditures can be done on a daily or weekly basis, and typical categories might include *housing expenses*, such as rent or mortgage payments and renters' or home-owners' insurance, *utilities*, such as gas, electric, and telephone bills as well as cable television, *food, personal and other household items, clothing, travel expenses*, such as vehicle payments, insurance, gas, maintenance, and repair, and *medical expenses. Entertainments or other unnecessary outlays, charitable donations, savings, debt repayment*, and *school expenses* are additional categories that might be considered in developing a budget. Each disbursement can be recorded within its given category and each category tallied on a regular basis to determine where financial means are being utilized.   One may then decide if reallocation is warranted, especially in instances where financial means are insufficient to meet one's needs. "Tightening one's belt"[90] is often easier than increasing one's income. Below is a grid that might be completed in determining allocation of expenditures for future budgeting purposes.

---

[90] origin and meaning cited on www.phrases.org.uk/meanings

Financial Allocation Chart

Housing	Utilities	Food	Personal &other household items	Clothing	Travel	Medical
Item Expense 1) 2) 3) etc.	Item expense 1) 2) 3) etc.	Item expense 1) 2) 3) etc.	Item expense 1) 2) 3) etc.	Item expense 1) 2) 3) etc.	Item expense 1) 2) 3) etc.	Item expense 1) 2) 3) etc.
Total $	Total $	Total $	Total $	Total $	Total $	Total $

Once a person has developed a clear understanding as to where financial resources are being expended, he or she can then determine if some adjustments are necessary in his or her spending patterns and how best to budget finances for future needs. Some expenses will be of a *fixed* amount and can be counted on to recur on a regular basis, such as a mortgage or rent payment. A person's budget will likely revolve around those expenditures. Other disbursements, however, will be of a more *flexible* nature, such as certain household items that may not be necessary for one's survival, and might have to be sacrificed in order to make all of the fixed outlays of money. A similar grid to the one above may be developed in assigning future resource. The sum total of the amounts devoted to the various categories should not exceed the finite amount available for budgeting. Otherwise, a financial deficit, or debt, will be accrued. In addition, one may plan into one's budget expenses that may not occur on a monthly basis, for instance, a quarterly insurance premium or a long-awaited vacation, for which a certain amount may be allotted from one's income on a biweekly or monthly basis in anticipation of the more distant expenditure.

Budget (finite $ amount based upon net income)

Housing	Utilities	Food	Personal & other household items	Clothing	Travel	Medical
Allotted amount $	Allotted amount $	Allotted amount $	Allotted amount $	Allotted amount $	Allotted amount $	Allotted amount $

Being a prudent wife may entail far more than merely budgeting one's monthly income. For example, a woman may determine to eat at home more often than to eat out in saving on food expenses or to repair an item of clothing that still has some good use in it rather than to buy new in saving on her clothing disbursement. Brainstorming methods of meeting one's needs where financial means may not always be available is a necessary talent in ensuring that she and her loved ones do not go without. Finances are such a critical aspect of a marriage relationship, and, regardless of how a woman allocates her dollar or makes it stretch, it is essential that she learn to live within her own means and those provided by her husband in aiding her support and that of her children.

An additional point might be considered in regard to being a prudent wife. In the scriptures, we are counseled,

> Let your families be small . . . as pertaining to those who do not belong to your families; That those things that are provided for you, to bring to pass my work, be not taken from you and given to those that are not worthy—And thereby you be

hindered in accomplishing those things which I have commanded you (D&C 90:25-27).[91]

In addition, "Thou shalt be diligent in preserving what thou hast, that thou mayest be a wise steward; for it is the free gift of the Lord thy God, and thou art his steward" (D&C 136:27).[92] Each woman may well take those words to heart in considering her priorities in life and in devoting her time, her energies, her financial resource, and talents to bettering her own home life and the lives of those who abide with her. So frequently, women feel compelled to allot their resources outside their own home environments, and often, that is to their detriment. Women must be wise in determining the best use of those things with which they have been blessed so that they might bless the lives of those for whom they are truly responsible, their husbands and their children.

A final story I'd like to relate in regard to prudential living was recounted to me by my father in reference to his dad. My paternal grandfather had the great misfortune of losing his mother to death at a very young age and of not being well accepted by her successor, his father's second wife. While his two younger siblings were allowed to remain in the home, he was "left to his own devices"[93] in making his way in this world. I was told by an aunt that he was a boy merely 12 years of age the first time he ventured forth to Alaska, that time as a cabin boy on a train, and that

---

[91] *The Doctrine and Covenants of the Church of Jesus Christ of Latter-Day Saints.*
[92] *The Doctrine and Covenants of the Church of Jesus Christ of Latter-Day Saints.*
[93] origin and meaning cited on www.phrases.org.uk/meanings

he was 18 years old when he again braved the vast expanse of the Alaskan wilderness to earn a living as one who delivered mail by dogsled during the years of the gold rush there. He built a cabin in which he could escape the harsh elements of the rugged terrain, and, while his daily sustenance was earned through honest endeavor with a reliable outcome, others around him dug away at the earth and panned for gold.

A certain old miner by the name of "Lucky" Charlie just happened to strike it rich in his quest for that most precious mineral and squandered all his earnings on riotous living. Penniless and without a place to call his own, he found shelter for a time with my grandfather in the cabin he had built with his own two hands, nestled by the warmth of his fire, and found nourishment in abiding with him. Each of those necessities of life was gained through my grandfather's daily exertions, not through a windfall of good luck like Charlie was wont to find.

It seems there is a lesson to be learned in making a comparison between those two men and their differing experiences and approaches to life. My grandfather's daily struggle brought with it a sound appreciation for life's little comforts, knowledge of what it meant to go without, and an understanding of others' misfortunes and desire to be of help to them. "Lucky" Charlie's desires had been only to land his fortune and to lavish it on idle pleasures and pursuits. Once down on his luck and shunned by those who had so recently befriended him in his brief *but exhaustive* outlay of funds, he, like the Prodigal Son (Luke 15:11-32),[94] sought for comfort

---

[94] *The Holy Bible.*

where it was to be found. Wisdom and safety lie in the things we can count on, our own efforts in making our way in this life, and not on fortune's fancy.

So, in a woman's quest for prudential living, she must pay careful attention to her family's allocation of financial resource, make necessary adjustments to spending patterns by developing and maintaining a feasible budget, and look for ways to live within her means and those provided by her husband. In addition, she must reserve for herself and her family those things necessary for their support and not squander them needlessly on associations or pursuits outside her immediate home environment. By so doing, she will enhance the degree of happiness and security to which she and her family can attain by helping to avoid debt and perhaps even by setting aside something in the way of savings for the unforeseen needs of tomorrow.

In considering some of your own observations and life experiences, what examples come to mind in which women have exercised prudence in their lives and in their relationships with the men they knew? Those may include, but are not limited to, interactions between parents, grandparents, aunts and uncles, neighbors, and friends.

_____

_____

_____

*How do you, as a woman, exercise prudence in your life
and in your interactions with the men you know?*

_____

_____

_____

_____

_____

_____

_____

_____

In what ways do you perceive you might improve?

_____

_____

_____

_____

_____

_____

_____

_____

_____

How might those improvements enhance your life and your relationships?

_____

_____

_____

_____

_____

_____

_____

_____

Be a Beacon.

Webster's definition of *beacon* is "any signal that serves to guide or orient, as a fire, a lighthouse, a radio beacon, etc." In the scriptures, we read,

> Ye are the light of the world. A city that is set on an hill cannot be hid. Neither do men light a candle, and put it under a bushel, but on a candlestick; and it giveth light unto all that are in the house. Let your light so shine before men, that they may see your good works, and glorify your

Father which is in heaven (Matthew 5:14-16;[95] 3 Nephi 12:14-16).[96]

A woman's example in the life of a man is of utmost importance in guiding him in the course she would have him go. To be an *example* is to be "one who or that which is proposed or is proper for imitation." An *exemplar* is that which demonstrates a "pattern to be copied or imitated." To be *exemplary* is to be "worthy of imitation; commendable." *To exemplify* is "to show or illustrate by example." Thus, a woman serves her own purposes well by exhibiting for the man in her life those characteristics which she hopes he will one day come to exemplify, *and what might those characteristics be?* The answer is quite simply anything her heart can imagine that would bring her joy.

Fulfilling callings.

For instance, a woman finds joy in fulfilling the callings bestowed upon her. Interactions with her spouse, her children, and others whom she holds dear are enhanced when "love is spoken" (pp. 190-191)[97] within her home. She may call her loved ones by endearments and find other ways to treat them with kindness. Caring for her household environment is another means of finding joy in her life and of setting a good example for her husband to follow. Maintaining clean and orderly surroundings can only enhance the

---

[95] *The Holy Bible.*

[96] *The Book of Mormon: Another Testament of Jesus Christ.*

[97] Corporation of the President of the Church of Jesus Christ of Latter-Day Saints. (1989). *Children's Songbook.* Salt Lake City, UT: Deseret Book Company.

peaceful and friendly atmosphere she hopes to create therein. In addition, the stalwart attitude *she* embraces in looking to the support of her family and meeting financial obligations will likely instill the same within *him*. Also, as she seeks joy though learning about and doing the things she loves, so will those who follow her lead.

As a married woman, I have noticed the influence my behavior has had upon my husband and others around me. For example, if I am kind, so will they be. If, however, I just happened to wake "up on the wrong side of the bed"[98] on any given morning and decided that yelling, screaming, throwing a fit, and criticizing everyone were "par for [my] course,"[99] I'd better be prepared to receive in return a healthy portion of what I just dished out as well as witness total chaos in the interactions between other members of my family. Remember the Golden Rule to "do unto others as you would have them do unto you,"[100] as based on the scriptural admonition in Matthew 7:12?[101] It is also a good idea to do unto others as you would have them do unto one another.

In regard to maintaining a clean and orderly home environment, the household where I grew up was not always a prime example of pristine living. However, my mother had been raised in a haven of cleanliness and order, and, seeing that my maternal grandmother lived only a block away, I frequented her household as a primary retreat from an otherwise chaotic home life.

---

[98] origin and meaning cited on www.phrases.org.uk/meanings
[99] origin and meaning cited on www.phrases.org.uk/meanings
[100] origin and meaning cited on www.phrases.org.uk/meanings
[101] *The Holy Bible.*

While I loved my parents dearly, going to Grandma's house was a treat that was much looked forward to, and the time I spent there instilled within me a great desire to imitate the lifestyle she exemplified. I also had the opportunity to practice employing some of my grandmother's skills. Cooking, washing dishes, and working in her garden and flowerbeds were means of learning important life tasks that would serve me well one day. While I am not always a perfect homemaker, at least I know the goal for which I am striving because I have seen it done so very well. Knowing that it's possible makes it seem that much more attainable to me.

When it comes to meeting financial obligations, my own work history has been stronger at certain points in my life than at others. That may be the case with anyone. However, I can definitely look to the example set by many of my progenitors in strengthening my own resolve to continue moving in a positive direction. My father traveled great distances for many years in an effort to support his family. Each of my brothers has also set a great example for me of industry in providing support and meeting financial obligations. Grandparents and great-grandparents alike have left a legacy detailing the meaning of hard work. With those and other examples to follow, hopefully, I can perpetuate a pattern that will have a meaningful impact on my own family as well. Again, having seen it done makes the goal that much more a reality.

Seeking joy through learning is another avenue through which a woman can exert her influence in her home. Doing the things that she loves is oftentimes the best way to set the tone therein. Some of the things I remember most about my grandmother were her hobbies, or avocations. She loved to care for plants, both those which grew within and those which grew without her household. In pots inside were exotic ferns and African violets. Along the foundation outside were more ferns, tulips, snapdragons, and lilies of the valley. Bridal-wreath, lilac, and snowball bushes adorned the outskirts of her property, while peonies and roses accented the garden. Names of many of the flowers evade me, but I still remember their bursts of color, reds, pinks, and oranges, yellows, whites, and purples, too, overflowing the hanging planters and planter boxes on the patio. I remember that geraniums, marigolds, and fuchsias were among them. Grandma could boast of having multiple beds dedicated solely to flowers directly behind her house and past the garden, near the river. I believe pansies, daffodils, and hyacinths were included in those, their delicate sweetness perfuming the air about them. In addition to the flowering plants were fruit-bearing trees (i.e., apple, cherry, peach, and pear) and bushes (i.e., gooseberry, blackcurrant, and raspberry), grapevines, and a garden that provided much of the sustenance for our family during the winter months. In addition to having a green thumb, Grandma was also a bird lover and had raised songbirds for many years. While that was before my day, my oldest brother and one of my cousins have often spoken fondly of their recollections of Grandma's talent at raising birds. Grandma also did beautiful handiwork, and examples were replete within her household when she died. No matter what a woman's particular interests and aptitudes may be, it is in the fulfillment of those through hobbies, or avocations, that she sets the example for others to follow.

A woman has the ability to set a good example by fulfilling the various callings in her life. Caring for her relationships, her home environment, her work commitments, and her avocations are all means of providing a pattern she hopes others will one day exemplify.

In considering some of your own observations and life experiences, what examples come to mind in which women have shown others the way in fulfilling callings in their lives and in their relationships with the men they knew? Those may include, but are not limited to, interactions between parents, grandparents, aunts and uncles, neighbors, and friends.

_____

_____

_____

_____

_____

_____

_____

_____

_____

How do you, as a woman, set an example of fulfilling callings in your life and in your interactions with the men you know?

_____

_____

_____

_____

_____

_____

_____

_____

_____

_____

In what ways do you perceive you might improve?

_____

_____

_____

_____

_____

_____

_____

_____

_____

How might those improvements enhance your life and your relationships?

_____

_____

_____

_____

_____

_____

_____

_____

_____

Being patient.

"Tribulation worketh patience; And patience, experience; and experience, hope: And hope maketh not ashamed" (Romans 5:3-5).[102] Has anyone failed to hear the adage that "patience is a virtue?"[103] It certainly is a characteristic worthy of emulation and for which each woman must strive. What does it mean to be *patient?* It entails "bearing pain or trial without complaining; sustaining afflictions with fortitude, calmness, or submission; waiting with calmness; not hasty; long-suffering; persevering; calmly diligent; able to bear" (Webster). *How might a woman's patient walk in bearing up under trials, tribulations, and hardships bring joy into her life and the lives of others around her?* Encountering difficulties in life is unavoidable. Each man and woman, boy and girl must endure the bad with the good, pain with pleasure, and ugliness

---

[102] *The Holy Bible.*
[103] origin and meaning cited on www.phrases.org.uk/meanings

with the beauty in life. There is no getting around that stark reality. However, there is great variability as to how each person will fare in that quest to gain experience, and watching and following in the footsteps of others who have done well is in part an assurance of success.

I have witnessed much in others' lives that has added to my own personal strength and inner resolve. I have seen the smiling face of a dear friend who was racked with cancer and soon to depart this world. Pain and sickness seemed to have little hold on him, and his sweetness, humility, and unparalleled bravery have sustained me through the minor aches and pains of my ordinary existence. I have watched the daily battle which my grandmother fought as she grieved the loss of her husband following his death. Waking each morning beside his empty place on their bed, preparing her solitary meals, and reaching out to the man who could no longer reach back to her were all part of her daily plight. As time progressed, her despair gradually faded, and she reemerged to find joy in life and in meeting the needs of her posterity once again, as she had so often done before. Two years following the death of her husband, her son died also, and she began the processes of grieving and healing once more. It is with reservation that I look to the future and the probability that I will face similar losses in my own life, but I am confident that my grandmother's example will help sustain me should my path at times fall into shadow before returning to the light. There is joy in knowing the strength and beauty with which others have survived the trials, the tribulations, and hardships life has so freely bestowed upon them and a quiet hope and calming reassurance that life goes on *whether we want it to or not.* As a woman sets an example of patience for others around her, she instills within the joy, the hope, and sweet assurance we all stand in need of as we face the challenges presented by each new day.

In considering some of your own observations and life experiences, what examples come to mind in which women have shown others the way in being patient in their lives and in their relationships with the men they knew? Those may include, but are not limited to, interactions between parents, grandparents, aunts and uncles, neighbors, and friends.

_____

_____

_____

_____

_____

_____

_____

_____

_____

How do you, as a woman, set an example of patience in your life and in your interactions with the men you know?

_____

_____

_____

_____

_____

_____

_____

_____

_____

In what ways do you perceive you might improve?

_____

_____

_____

_____

_____

_____

_____

_____

How might those improvements enhance your life and your relationships?

_____

_____

_____

_____

_____

_____

_____

_____

_____

Being happy.

There is sunshine in my soul today,
More glorious and bright
Than glows in any earthly sky,
For Jesus is my light.
Oh, there's sunshine, blessed sunshine
When the peaceful happy moments roll.
When Jesus shows his smiling face,
There is sunshine in the soul.

There is music in my soul today,
A carol to my King,
And Jesus listening can hear
The songs I cannot sing.
Oh, there's sunshine, blessed sunshine
When the peaceful happy moments roll.
When Jesus shows his smiling face,
There is sunshine in the soul.

There is springtime in my soul today,
For when the Lord is near,
The dove of peace sings in my heart,
The flow'rs of grace appear.
Oh, there's sunshine, blessed sunshine
When the peaceful happy moments roll.

When Jesus shows his smiling face,
There is sunshine in the soul.

There is gladness in my soul today,
And hope and praise and love,
For blessings which he gives me now,
For joys "laid up" above.
Oh, there's sunshine, blessed sunshine
When the peaceful happy moments roll.
When Jesus shows his smiling face,
There is sunshine in the soul (hymn no. 227).[104]

Happiness is synonymous with *joy*, or "excitement or pleasurable feeling caused by the acquisition or expectation of good" (Webster). The scriptures counsel, "Men are, that they might have joy" (2 Nephi 2:25),[105] and joy is most easily attained when we see light emanating from others around us. It is a contagious influence for bringing about much good in our lives. An outward display of happiness, such as a simple smile on a woman's face, may cause others around her, including the man in her life, to wonder and inquire about her own personal formula for finding joy. She may then have the opportunity to share it. The scriptures counsel her to "*be* ready always to *give* an answer to every man that asketh you a reason of the hope that is in you" (1 Peter 3:15).[106] For me, happiness comes from fulfilling my life's responsibilities to the very best of my ability, from holding fond associations with those whom I love, and

---

[104] Corporation of the President of the Church of Jesus Christ of Latter-Day Saints. (1985). *Hymns of the Church of Jesus Christ of Latter-Day Saints.* Salt Lake City, UT: Deseret Book Company.
[105] *The Book of Mormon: Another Testament of Jesus Christ.*
[106] *The Holy Bible.*

from seeking a calm assurance that my offerings are accepted of the Lord. Others around me do seem to notice the smile on my face and will often mention that it gives them a lift as well.

What brings happiness into your life, and how might you best share that with others around you?

_____

_____

_____

_____

_____

_____

_____

_____

_____

The truest example of happiness set by anyone I have ever known was that of my father. He was the life of any party. He was a party in and of himself. At every holiday, he would beam with delight and encourage others to do likewise. He was a jolly Santa Claus every day of the year. He would come home from work each night and open his arms to my older brother and me when we were small children. We would run to him, be lifted up, and told to wrap our arms around his neck and try our very hardest to squeeze the life out of him. He would invariably turn a bright shade of red, and his "five o'clock shadow"[107] never failed to leave our tender cheeks reddened as well. Mom would always chide him for that. Dad enjoyed pulling us around the block in our little red wagon just as much as we relished being pulled in it. How we loved our father, and what joy he brought into our lives with his constant state of happiness. He and my mother may not always have hit it off on every point, but one thing they had in common was the joy they both felt when Dad joked around with her and made her laugh. Though he preceded her in death by a number of years, memories of his humor kept her laughing practically 'til her dying day. What an example he was for me and what a legacy I can pass on to others around me if only I will follow his lead.

The scriptures have counseled each woman to "keep house, *and to be* a joyful mother of children" (Psalms 113:9),[108] to "be glad and rejoice" (Revelations 19:7),[109] to "lift up your hearts and rejoice" (D&C 42:69),[110] and, in numerous places, to "be of good cheer." As each woman fulfills the responsibilities of her life with joy, she, too, can be a contagious influence for good and bring happiness into the lives of others around her, *but how is it that she attains such gladness?* She, herself, can look to the examples set by others who have found their own recipes for bringing joy into their lives and those around them. She may simply watch and observe the things that they say and do, or she may venture forth to inquire about any secret ingredients

---

[107] origin and meaning cited on www.phrases.org.uk/meanings

[108] *The Holy Bible.*

[109] *The Holy Bible.*

[110] *The Doctrine and Covenants of the Church of Jesus Christ of Latter-Day Saints.*

which underlie their success. Those who have attained that degree of happiness in their own lives are usually willing to share what they have learned with others. As a matter of fact, I believe it is the very act of sharing and of giving that is at the heart of feeling so much joy.

In considering some of your own observations and life experiences, what examples come to mind in which women have shown others the way in being happy in their lives and in their relationships with the men they knew? Those may include, but are not limited to, interactions between parents, grandparents, aunts and uncles, neighbors, and friends.

_____

_____

_____

_____

_____

_____

_____

_____

_____

How do you, as a woman, set an example of happiness in your life and in your interactions with the men you know?

_____

_____

_____

_____

_____

_____

_____

_____

_____

_____

In what ways do you perceive you might improve?

_____

_____

_____

_____

_____

_____

_____

_____

How might those improvements enhance your life and your relationships?

_____

_____

_____

125

_____

_____

_____

_____

_____

_____

Being pleasant.

To be *pleasant* is to give "pleasure to the mind or to the senses," and *pleasure*, like happiness, is "the feeling produced by the enjoyment or expectation of good" (Webster). When I think about the things that give me pleasure, I can imagine in my mind a fragrant field, the warmth of the sunshine on my skin, Grandma's chocolate cake, and birds singing in the breeze. I see the faces of my infant grandson and his two older sisters smiling at me and sense happiness from their abiding love. The strength of my husband's arms around me and the gentleness of his touch are what I long for as we come together at the end of each day spent apart.

Now, *in what way does a woman bring pleasure into the life of a man, and how does she please his mind and his senses?* Men, too, like women, enjoy the physical pleasure engendered by touch, and, as has been spoken of before, a woman's touch is a great comfort in the life of a man. However, *beyond the avenue of physical intimacy, how is it that a woman comes to gratify and to satisfy the heart and the mind of her male companion?* I believe it is through the disposition with

126

which she conducts herself in her interactions with him. A *disposition* is a "temper or emotional constitution of the mind" (Webster). To be of a pleasant disposition is to be amiable or agreeable in one's conduct toward another.

It seems a small thing for a man to ask of a woman that she merely be amiable or agreeable in her interactions with him, but troubles of large proportions can arise should she choose not to comply. One might remember the sorry end to the story of King David and his first wife, Michal, or consider the sad consequences of my waking "up on the wrong side of the bed" on any given morning. Seemingly small acts can have far-reaching effects. Therefore, it is wise to choose one's actions carefully, including the manner in which we treat others. "What's good for the goose is good for the gander,"[111] and where love is given the same is received. Therein, joy abounds.

How does a woman develop a pleasant disposition? First, she needs to gauge others' responses to her characteristic way of interacting with them. If she is one who tends to say or do things that at times get on others' nerves, irritate, or annoy them, she may first want to consider simply refraining from speaking those words or engaging in those actions which have made her culpable in any way. Next, she may benefit from looking to the example of those who have seemingly engendered others' high regard or opinion. By following their lead, she may learn to exemplify characteristics which have won them approval rather than disdain. Smiling, showing interest in others by

---

[111] origin and meaning cited on www.phrases.org.uk/meanings

asking them questions that are not too personal or probing, responding politely when approached or spoken to, and being generally kind are likely examples of those traits. Speaking words like "please" and "thank you" goes a long way toward instilling genuine regard in others for us, and, if a woman's typical approach to relating with others wins their favor rather than their disapproval, she might continue on her current course with the assurance that her own example is worthy of emulation.

In considering some of your own observations and life experiences, what examples come to mind in which women have shown others the way in being pleasant in their lives and in their relationships with the men they knew? Those may include, but are not limited to, interactions between parents, grandparents, aunts and uncles, neighbors, and friends.

_____

_____

_____

_____

_____

_____

_____

_____

_____

How do you, as a woman, set an example of pleasantness in your life and in your interactions with the men you know?

_____

_____

_____

_____

_____

_____

_____

_____

_____

In what ways do you perceive you might improve?

_____

_____

_____

_____

_____

_____

_____

_____

_____

How might those improvements enhance your life and your relationships?

_____

_____

_____

_____

_____

_____

_____

_____

_____

Being thankful.

To be *thankful* is to be "expressive of gratitude; grateful; appreciative" (Webster). The scriptures counsel, "Be ye thankful" (Colossians 3:15),[112] "Cease not to give thanks" (Ephesians 1:16),[113] "In every thing give thanks" (1 Thessalonians 5:18[114]; D&C 98:1),[115] and "Give thanks in all things" (Mosiah 26:39).[116] Joy is found in the expression of gratitude and appreciation for life's many blessings and for those whom we love. It is a most important part of a relationship between a man and a woman, and the one who takes the initiative

---

[112] *The Holy Bible.*

[113] *The Holy Bible.*

[114] *The Holy Bible.*

[115] *The Doctrine and Covenants of the Church of Jesus Christ of Latter-Day Saints.*

[116] *The Book of Mormon: Another Testament of Jesus Christ.*

in relaying such sentiment will be a likely recipient of the same and of many of life's good things. I am fortunate to have a husband who often recounts the things in life for which he is grateful and doubly fortunate to be included among them. He praises my efforts to care for our home environment and for all who dwell therein, to comfort him in times of stress or despair, sickness and pain, and to endeavor to assist him in procuring a means of support for our family. He tells me that I'm "kind" and "beautiful" and that he's "lucky" to have me in his life. His thankful declarations instill much of the same goodwill within me, and I cannot help but to feel blessed at having such a wonderful and loving husband to comfort and uphold me. Neither can I withhold those thoughts from him. As my husband communicates his love for me through his many expressions of gratitude, I am also filled with the desire to speak my love and thanks unto him. It is a circle that cannot be broken except by occasional neglect to attend to our debt of gratitude to those whom we love.

Verbal expressions are only one means of relaying appreciation to others for the good they do unto us, whether we choose to relay our thanks through the spoken or the written word. We can also reward others by returning one kind deed for another, by offering small tokens of appreciation in the form of gifts, or by spending a few precious moments of our time with them. Especially in regard to loving relationships between men and women, expressions of gratitude can be offered in some form of physical intimacy, such as a kiss or a hug. Those gestures are also very acceptable and highly appreciated means of expressing gratitude between parents and children, other family members, and close friends.   Through whatever channel we choose to express our appreciation, thanksgiving tends to flow back to us as we set an example for others to follow in showing them our thanks and gratitude.

In considering some of your own observations and life experiences, what examples come to mind in which women have shown others the way in being thankful in their lives and in their relationships with the men they knew?   Those may include, but are not limited to, interactions between parents, grandparents, aunts and uncles, neighbors, and friends.

_____

_____

_____

_____

_____

_____

_____

_____

_____

How do you, as a woman, set an example of thankfulness in your life and in your interactions with the men you know?

_____

_____

_____

_____

_____

_____

_____

_____

_____

In what ways do you perceive you might improve?

_____

_____

_____

_____

_____

_____

_____

_____

How might those improvements enhance your life and your relationships?

_____

_____

_____

_____

Forgiving.

"To forgive is divine."[117] _To forgive_ is "to cease to
feel resentment against; to give up a claim on account
of; to grant remission of an offense, debt, fine, or
penalty; to pardon; to free from the consequences of an
injurious act or crime" (Webster). To have a divine
nature is to possess godlike qualities, and the mercy
entailed in forgiveness is none other than divine. In
regard to one who has sorrowed for sin and has put past
deeds behind him in exchange for a brighter and more
hopeful tomorrow, the scriptures counsel, "All his
transgressions that he hath committed, they shall not be
mentioned unto him" (Ezekiel 18:22)[118] and again,
"None of his sins that he hath committed shall be
mentioned unto him" (Ezekiel 33:16).[119] We are told,
"Forgive, and ye shall be forgiven" (Luke 6:37)[120] and,
"If thy brother . . . repent, forgive him" (Luke 17:3).[121]
Pertaining to one who grieves for sin, we are taught,
"Ye _ought_ . . . to forgive _him_, and comfort _him_, lest
perhaps such a one should be swallowed up with

---

[117] origin and meaning cited on www.phrases.org.uk/meanings
[118] _The Holy Bible._
[119] _The Holy Bible._
[120] _The Holy Bible._
[121] _The Holy Bible._

overmuch sorrow. Wherefore I beseech you that ye would confirm *your* love toward him" (2 Corinthians 2:7-8).[122] Instruction is given that we be "kind one to another, tenderhearted, forgiving one another, even as God for Christ's sake hath forgiven you" (Ephesians 4:32).[123] We are also advised,

> Put on therefore, as the elect of God, holy and beloved, bowels of mercies, kindness, humbleness of mind, meekness, longsuffering; Forbearing one another, and forgiving one another, if any man have a quarrel against any: even as Christ forgave you, so also *do* ye (Colossians 3:12-13).[124]

Additionally, we are exhorted, if any "confess his sins before thee and me, and repenteth in the sincerity of his heart, him shall ye forgive, and I [God] will forgive him also" (Mosiah 26:29).[125] A final note of warning is offered:

> I, the Lord, will forgive whom I will forgive, but of you it is required to forgive all men. And ye ought to say in your hearts—let God judge between me and thee, and reward thee according to thy deeds (D&C 64:10-11).[126]

What an act of faith is required to leave all judgment in God's hands.

---

[122] *The Holy Bible.*

[123] *The Holy Bible.*

[124] *The Holy Bible.*

[125] *The Book of Mormon: Another Testament of Jesus Christ.*

[126] *The Doctrine and Covenants of the Church of Jesus Christ of Latter-Day Saints.*

How does forgiveness pertain to the relationship between a man and a woman? I, for one, know the anguish of holding onto past resentments and feelings of bitterness toward others for wrongs they have committed against me, especially those of the opposite sex who have hurt me or seemingly betrayed my trust. An inability to bypass feelings of pain and betrayal has created an impasse beyond which no further progress could be made in a given relationship, and the greater likelihood was that the union came to an end. It is true there are some wounds that are all but impossible to heal from and that sometimes healing is best accomplished on one's own, apart from the source of one's misery. However, if one is to continue to reside with another in a partnership and circumstances are such that *he* and *she* can overcome the minor ups and downs of any normal coupling, forgiveness is the pinnacle to which we must attain, for no one is perfect and we all stand in need of pardon from time to time. There is nothing more miserable than abiding in the presence of one who cannot forgive and nothing more joyful than basking in the mercy of one who can.

Jesus, though not known to have coupled with anyone during his mortal ministry, forgave many men and women of the wrongs they committed while in mortality. While healing "a man sick of the palsy," Jesus said unto him, "Son, be of good cheer; thy sins be forgiven thee" (Matthew 9:2).[127] In regard to the "woman taken in adultery" (John 8:3),[128] Jesus said, "He that is without sin among you, let him first cast a stone at her" (John 8:7)[129] and "Neither do I condemn

---

[127] *The Holy Bible.*
[128] *The Holy Bible.*
[129] *The Holy Bible.*

thee: go, and sin no more" (John 8:11).[130] As pertaining to the soldiers who crucified him, Jesus asked, "Father, forgive them; for they know not what they do" (Luke 23:34).[131] What a fitting end to a mortal life so replete with forgiveness and charity.

Who among women can follow that example in coming to forgive the many weaknesses and shortcomings that are so abundant in mankind? I would say she is a woman with the world at her fingertips and one who can command the best her man has to offer, his undying love and appreciation for all she has given him and the joy of knowing she has forgiven him, *but how is such forgiveness possible?* Perhaps a fitting place to begin might be for her to stop and think about the many mistakes she has made in her own life and of times when she has been forgiven. Such remembrances are an opportunity to relive the humility attending our own imperfections, and such humility is essential in looking to the needs of others for our forgiveness and in placing their needs before our own feelings of pride or selfishness.

I remember a time when I was a very small child and had wandered into the garden of an elderly gentleman in my neighborhood to help myself to some of his most delectable peas. I picked them from his garden and was in the very act of pilfering when he happened upon me. Though being very young, I must have known of the wrongfulness of my actions because I feared the consequences of being caught. However, instead of reprimanding me for the impropriety of my

---

[130] *The Holy Bible.*
[131] *The Holy Bible.*

deeds, Mr. Bailey, *Wonderful Mr. Bailey*, grasped my little hands in his and filled them with peas from his garden. *What a kind and loving man he was to me, and how very thankful I was for his forgiveness and generosity.* Though consequences for sin are often necessary in training both children and adults in the basics of right versus wrong, I have to wonder how different our world might be if there were more love and forgiveness for those who stray and less resentment and rejection from those who have been wronged.

In considering some of your own observations and life experiences, what examples come to mind in which women have shown others the way in forgiving in their lives and in their relationships with the men they knew? Those may include, but are not limited to, interactions between parents, grandparents, aunts and uncles, neighbors, and friends.

_____

_____

_____

_____

_____

_____

_____

_____

_____

How do you, as a woman, set an example of forgiveness in your life and in your interactions with the men you know?

_____

_____

_____

_____

_____

_____

_____

_____

In what ways do you perceive you might improve?

_____

_____

_____

_____

_____

_____

_____

_____

How might those improvements enhance your life and your relationships?

_____

_____

_____

_____

_____

_____

_____

_____

Setting an example is a burden from which no man or woman can escape, for others are constantly looking on. There is no way of avoiding that. One may be seen as a beacon in life's storms, a jagged rock bathed in raging waters, or anything in between. To each of us is given a choice to be "a city that is set on an hill" (Matthew 5:14;[132] 3 Nephi 12:14),[133] a dark abyss, or simply someone who is not trying to make much of a difference in either regard, or, in other words, "salt that hath lost its savor" (Matthew 5:13;[134] Luke 14:34;[135] 3 Nephi 12:13;[136] 3 Nephi 16:15;[137] D&C 101:39-40;[138]

---

[132] *The Holy Bible.*

[133] *The Book of Mormon: Another Testament of Jesus Christ.*

[134] *The Holy Bible.*

[135] *The Holy Bible.*

[136] *The Book of Mormon: Another Testament of Jesus Christ.*

[137] *The Book of Mormon: Another Testament of Jesus Christ.*

D&C 103:9-10).[139] The impact we will have on others is one of the more crucial decisions we will make in this life and one which must be repeated with about the same frequency as each new breath or every step we take. To be a beacon in the home entails many things. Included among those are a few that have been briefly touched upon in this chapter. The manner in which we fulfill our callings and bear up under the trials and tribulations set before us as well as attempt to be happy, pleasant, thankful, and forgiving on a fairly constant basis are means by which we might show others the way we would have them go, especially the men in our lives. After all, in our quest for joy, "the unbelieving husband is sanctified by the wife, and the unbelieving wife is sanctified by the husband" (1 Corinthians 7:14;[140] D&C 74:1).[141]

Never Leave Him.

A final note of counsel given in behalf of a woman who intends to live long and well with the man whom she has chosen as her life's partner is that she must never leave him *saving for the gravest of offense.* She is told, "Where your treasure is, there will your heart be also" (Matthew 6:21;[142] Luke 12:34;[143] 3 Nephi 13:21).[144] I would caution a woman to treasure her

---

[138] *The Doctrine and Covenants of the Church of Jesus Christ of Latter-Day Saints.*

[139] *The Doctrine and Covenants of the Church of Jesus Christ of Latter-Day Saints.*

[140] *The Holy Bible.*

[141] *The Doctrine and Covenants of the Church of Jesus Christ of Latter-Day Saints.*

[142] *The Holy Bible.*

[143] *The Holy Bible.*

[144] *The Book of Mormon: Another Testament of Jesus Christ.*

husband and to do all within her means to bolster his efforts to treasure her as well. Once a man and a woman have chosen to devote their lives to one another, it behooves them both to overlook the minor flaws that may eat away at their mutual happiness and, instead, to concentrate their attentions on their partner's more admirable characteristics that may enhance their wedded bliss.

In regard to my own parents' marriage, a seeming impasse was reached within only about a year of their living together. My father's employment required that he relocate a fair distance from my mother's place of origin, the home where she was raised and where extended family and friends still resided and offered comfort and support to her in the early days of her life with my father and her young motherhood. Her reluctance to take her baby and leave her home, her extended family, and friends to join him in his efforts to support their own new family left my father with little recourse but to threaten the demise of their relationship. Mom was placed in a position of having to choose between living at home with her parents or moving away with her husband, a choice that seemingly should have been made at the marriage alter a year previously. Mom made the right decision, in my opinion, and joined Dad in his quest to make a living, though his career choices required them to relocate a number of times before finally settling down once again in my mother's hometown. Dad's vagabond lifestyle was one of the minor flaws Mom had to learn to forgive during their early years together, but his kind and caring disposition and his unparalleled sense of humor were characteristics that not only drew her to him initially but kept the two of them bonded throughout decades of daily ups and downs that are "par for the course" in any marriage relationship.

Through the scriptures, we are counseled, "Let not the wife depart from *her* husband . . . and let not the husband put away *his* wife" (1 Corinthians 7:10-11),[145] for "neither is the man without the woman, neither the woman without the man, in the Lord" (1 Corinthians 11:11).[146] Again, we are told, "*It is* not good that . . . man should be alone" (Genesis 2:18;[147] Moses 3:18;[148] Abraham 5:14)[149] and that he should "live joyfully with the wife whom [he] lovest" (Ecclesiastes 9:9).[150] God seems especially pleased with societies wherein "husbands love their wives, and . . . wives love their husbands" (Jacob 3:7).[151] He has counseled man, "Thou shalt love thy wife with all thy heart, and shalt cleave unto her and none else" (D&C 42:22).[152] How is it possible for man to cleave unto woman unless she, too, cleaves unto him? God has counseled women "to love their husbands" (Titus 2:4).[153]

As noted before, it is only for the gravest of offense that a woman might consider leaving the man to whom she is bound. *Infidelity*, *abuse*, and *an abiding unwillingness to provide a means of support* for himself

---

[145] *The Holy Bible.*

[146] *The Holy Bible.*

[147] *The Holy Bible.*

[148] *The Pearl of Great Price.*

[149] *The Pearl of Great Price.*

[150] *The Holy Bible.*

[151] *The Book of Mormon: Another Testament of Jesus Christ.*

[152] *The Doctrine and Covenants of the Church of Jesus Christ of Latter-Day Saints.*

[153] *The Holy Bible.*

143

and his family are the three "deadly sins"[154] of which I speak. A woman who has devoted herself to a man cannot but expect the same degree of loyalty from him. Anything less than complete fidelity is a betrayal of the trust which hangs so delicately in the balance of their union and is widely accepted justification for departing such a relationship. Man is counseled, "Rejoice with the wife of thy youth" (Proverbs 5:18)[155] and "Let none deal treacherously against" her (Malachi 2:15).[156] What man worth keeping would sell his birthright for a bowl of pottage (Genesis 25:29-34),[157] or betray the woman to whom he is committed for a minor dalliance?

Abuse, in any of its many forms, is also a grave infraction of trust. It is something that eats away at the heart of its tender victim often long years after the cruelty has ceased. Misguided words and actions live on in memory until such a time as one who is wounded may give way for a measure of healing to seep in. Certainly, continuing to abide in an abusive relationship is ill advised at best and more likely a sure means of destroying one's happiness and the potential success of one's partnership. Man is counseled, "He that troubleth his own house shall inherit the wind" (Proverbs 11:29).[158] Therefore, he must cease to disturb or be "left to his own devices" and "to kick against the pricks" (Acts 9:5;[159] 26:14;[160] D&C 121:38).[161]

---

[154] distinct from the seven deadly sins of Catholicism

[155] *The Holy Bible.*

[156] *The Holy Bible.*

[157] *The Holy Bible.*

[158] *The Holy Bible.*

[159] *The Holy Bible.*

[160] *The Holy Bible.*

[161] *The Doctrine and Covenants of the Church of Jesus Christ of Latter-Day Saints.*

Finally, who among men is not expected to provide a means of support for himself and his family? No man that I am aware of, saving for those who may be impaired in some way either physically or mentally, is free from society's expectations that he carry the temporal burden of sustaining his own life as well as the lives of those whom he loves. The scriptures counsel, "If any provide not for his own, and specially for those of his own house, he hath denied the faith, and is worse than an infidel" (1 Timothy 5:8)[162] and "Every man . . . is obliged to provide for his own family" (D&C 75:28)[163] and to "rule . . . well his own house" (1 Timothy 3:4).[164] "Women have claim on their husbands for their maintenance" (D&C 83:2),[165] and "children have claim upon their parents" (D&C 83:4).[166] Even Jacob, after having labored long years in the service of his father-in-law, Laban, asked, "When shall I provide for mine own house also" (Genesis 30:30)?[167] Only those so invested in the temporal support of their families truly stake a claim therein.

Certainly, there may be some *recourse* for the marriage relationship that has veered *off course* due to infidelity, abuse, or abandonment of one's temporal responsibilities. I have heard it said that, while a woman *or a man* may be justified in terminating her *or his* partnership under given conditions, it is better to

---

[162] *The Holy Bible.*

[163] *The Doctrine and Covenants of the Church of Jesus Christ of Latter-Day Saints.*

[164] *The Holy Bible.*

[165] *The Doctrine and Covenants of the Church of Jesus Christ of Latter-Day Saints.*

[166] *The Doctrine and Covenants of the Church of Jesus Christ of Latter-Day Saints.*

[167] *The Holy Bible.*

remain faithful to one's commitment if the relationship is in any way salvageable. It may be that "the unbelieving husband [can be] sanctified by the wife, and the unbelieving wife [can be] sanctified by the husband" (1 Corinthians 7:14;[168] D&C 74:1).[169] Perhaps there are means, such as counseling, to instill within the transgressor a commitment to change. However, in situations where one's own happiness, safety, and wellbeing are at stake, as well as those of one's children, the decision to remain in less than optimum circumstances must be made with the utmost care.

Saving for the three "deadly sins" of which I have spoken, most ups and downs in a given marriage relationship can be anticipated as being "par for the course," like my father's vagabond lifestyle during the early days of his union with my mother. No man or woman, when pairing his or her own life with that of another, will find any coupling completely free of difficulty, for no two people are exactly alike and differences invariably breed for contention. It is in learning to accept *and even embrace* the hardships that accompany those differences that we tend to grow as people both in our individual development as well as in our couple's interactions. Far be it for anyone to cast to the wind his or her greatest opportunities for personal growth through growing closer to and accommodating the needs of those whom we love. One may strive to make his or her wants known and, yet, willingly set them aside in favor of the good of the other or of the relationship. That is the pinnacle to which we must

---

[168] *The Holy Bible.*

[169] *The Doctrine and Covenants of the Church of Jesus Christ of Latter-Day Saints.*

146

attain, to be willing to sacrifice our own wants in behalf of another.

In considering some of your own observations and life experiences, what examples come to mind in which women have steadfastly abided by the men in their lives despite the minor ups and downs which are a natural part of a couple's relationship? Those may include, but are not limited to, interactions between parents, grandparents, aunts and uncles, neighbors, and friends.

_____

_____

_____

_____

_____

_____

_____

_____

_____

How do you, as a woman, if in a committed relationship with a man, steadfastly abide by him despite the minor ups and downs which are a natural part of your relationship?

_____

_____

_____

_____

_____

_____

_____

_____

_____

In what ways do you perceive you might improve?

_____

_____

_____

_____

_____

_____

_____

_____

How might those improvements enhance your life and your relationship?

_____

_____

_____

_____

_____

_____

_____

_____

_____

Contained within the pages of this chapter are many points of instruction to assist women in their daily sojourn with the men whom they love. Though no single notion may be considered more or less important than another in a general sense, one or more of the ideas that have been related might be of special significance for a given partnership. Allowing a man to shine within his own specific realm, finding the wisdom in his counsel, being the soft touch in his otherwise adamant world, being prudent, setting the example she would have him follow, and steadfastly standing beside him are means by which a woman may gain an everlasting place beside the man whom she holds dear. Small are the sacrifices compared with the rewards inherent in such an endeavor, but great is the wisdom of those who show forth a willingness to embark upon the journey.

Conclusion

Though this book had no specific outline at its conception, the writer acknowledges that the ideas contained herein have fallen into three distinct parts, those being: 1) a woman's becoming something within herself, 2) a woman's building something outside herself, and 3) a woman's willingness to bend the knee somewhat in submitting herself to meet the needs of her partner as she engages in her union with a man. The *virtues* of womanhood are many and diverse and may each play a role in her pursuit of happiness through her own individual endeavors as well as those intentioned to bring joy into the lives of others. A woman's *responsibilities* in life are equally numerous and varied and must be attended to as she prepares herself for the added obligations inherent in marriage and parenthood. Primary among her duties is the sacred trust she owes her husband in *meeting his needs* as he cares for those of her and her children. *She* assists *him* in carrying the weight inherent in bringing forth society's successive generations, and *he* aids *her*. In developing herself, her lifestyle, and her ability to meet the needs of her partner and others who depend so heavily upon her, she is taking the steps necessary to emerge into mature womanhood, a quest that may take a lifetime to realize, to perfect, and to fully appreciate. As each woman embarks upon her journey and continues on her way, I wish her well and hope that some of the suggestions contained herein may be of help to her *if only in some small way.* Remember "that by small and simple things are great things brought to pass" (Alma 37:6).[170]

---

[170] *The Book of Mormon: Another Testament of Jesus Christ.*

www.ingramcontent.com/pod-product-compliance
Lightning Source LLC
Chambersburg PA
CBHW072123280526
45788CB00002B/522